WHEN MINISTRY IS MESSY

WHEN MINISTRY IS MESSY

·PRACTICAL SOLUTIONS TO DIFFICULT PROBLEMS·

Richard C. Brown, PH.D.

ST. ANTHONY MESSENGER PRESS
Cincinnati, Ohio

Scripture passages have been taken from *New Revised Standard Version Bible,* copyright ©1989 by the Division of Christian Education of the National Council of the Churches of Christ in the U.S.A., and used by permission. All rights reserved.

Cover and book design by Mark Sullivan.
Cover painting by Fr. Jim Van Vurst, O.F.M.

LIBRARY OF CONGRESS CATALOGING-IN-PUBLICATION DATA

Brown, Richard C., 1935-
  When ministry is messy : practical solutions to difficult problems / Richard C. Brown.
    p. cm.
  Includes bibliographical references.
  ISBN-13: 978-0-86716-777-1 (pbk. : alk. paper)
  ISBN-10: 0-86716-777-7 (pbk. : alk. paper)
  1. Pastoral theology. 2. Problem solving—Religious aspects—Christianity. I. Title.

BV4011.3.B78 2006
253—dc22

                                        2006014515

ISBN-13: 978-0-86716-777-1
ISBN-10: 0-86716-777-7

Published by St. Anthony Messenger Press
28 W. Liberty St.
Cincinnati, OH 45202
www.AmericanCatholic.org

Printed in the United States of America.

Printed on acid-free paper.

06 07 08 09 10 5 4 3 2 1

FOREWORD . . . . *ix*

INTRODUCTION. *1*

CHAPTER ONE: AN OVERVIEW OF CONFLICT IN MINISTRY *5*

[6] • Ministry Conflict—Three Causes and Possible Solutions
Natural Personality Differences
Emotional Illness
Sin

CHAPTER TWO: JESUS' APPROACH TO CONFLICT IN MATTHEW 23 . . . . *15*

[15] • Do Whatever They Teach—Natural Personality Differences
[16] • Woe to You, Blind Guides!—Emotional Illness
[17] • Full of Greed and Self-indulgence—Sin
[18] • The Greatest…Will Be Your Servant—Loving Servanthood
[20] • For Which is Greater—Logic
[20] • As a Hen Gathers Her Brood—Loving Forgiveness
[22] • The City That Kills the Prophets—Choosing to "Stay Stuck" in Conflict

CHAPTER THREE: NATURAL PERSONALITY DIFFERENCES *25*

[25] • The Value of Identifying Personality Skills
[28] • Identifying Personality Skills
[31] • How Natural Personality Skills Cause Conflict
[32] • Twelve Skills and How They Cause Conflict

CHAPTER FOUR: EMOTIONAL ILLNESS . . . *39*

[39] • The Behaviors of Emotional Illness
[41] • The Impact of Emotional Illness Behaviors on Victims
[42] • The Impact of Emotional Illness Behaviors on Ministries
[43] • The Need to Avoid Overreaction to Single Instances

[44] • Insufficient Reactions by Observers of the Emotionally Ill

[44] • How the Emotionally Ill Get Past Evaluations

CHAPTER FIVE: SIN 47

[48] • Lists of Sins from Saints Paul and Thomas Aquinas

[48] • Prioritizing the Sins That Cause the Most Harm to Ministry

Pride—The Primary Gateway to Harming Ministry

Injustice—Firing and Poor Hiring Practices

Scandal—Lust, Greed and Other Addictions

Lack of Courage—Lack of Ministry Protection

Sloth—Procrastination and Negligence

Factions—Source of Destructive Power

Unjust Accusations—Acting on False Information

Envy and Hatred—Source of Other Harmful Sins

Slander and Lies—Behavior That Destroys

Enmity and Strife—The Infighting

CHAPTER SIX: LOVING SERVANTHOOD . . 61

[61] • Loving Servanthood in Scripture

[63] • Servanthood as the Practical Application of Loving Your Neighbor

[64] • God's Servanthood Toward Us

[65] • Thankfulness and Humility—Corollaries to Servanthood

[67] • Servanthood as a Preference for the Poor

[68] • Servanthood as a Solution to Each of the Three Causes of Conflict

[68] • Practical Applications for Servanthood in Ministry Conflict Spirituality

[69] • Some Difficulties in Servanthood

CHAPTER SEVEN: LOGIC 73

[74] • The Importance of Logic in Spirituality

[76] • Logic's Place in Scripture

[77] • Petitioning for Light and Strength—the Corollary to Logic

[78] • Practical Applications of Logic in Ministry Conflict Spirituality
[78] • Logic as a Solution to Each of the Three Causes of Conflict

CHAPTER EIGHT: LOVING FORGIVENESS . . . 81
[82] • The Importance of Loving Forgiveness in Scripture
[87] • Gratitude and Petition for Help—Corollaries of Loving
       Forgiveness
[88] • Practical Applications of Loving Forgiveness in Ministry
       Conflict Spirituality
[89] • Loving Forgiveness as a Solution to the Three Causes of
       Conflict

CHAPTER NINE: "STAYING STUCK" AND
"SPEAKING UP" 91
[91] • How We "Stay Stuck" Today
[92] • Putting God on the Cross
[92] • Why We "Stay Stuck"
[93] • Why "Staying Stuck" Results in the Desire to Kill the Prophet
[94] • Jesus "Speaks Up"
[95] • Other Solutions to "Staying Stuck"
[96] • Practical Applications for "Speaking Up" in Ministry Conflict
       Spirituality

CHAPTER TEN: THE MINISTRY CONFLICT
SPIRITUALITY OF JESUS 99
[100] • What Is Spirituality?
[100] • Practicing God's Will and Joy Through Our Talents
[101] • Responding to God's Physical Creation
[101] • Gifts and Fruits of the Holy Spirit
[102] • The Mass and Sacraments
[103] • The Rest of Daily Life
[104] • Why the Ministry Conflict? Why the Cross?

BIBLIOGRAPHY 107

INDEX 113

FOREWORD

Back in the good old days—the old, old days—the question of the parish staff didn't arise. There was the pastor (often a monsignor) and the people who worked for him: the housekeeper, the cook, the engineer, the sister superior, the secretary and, last but certainly not least, the assistant pastors. They all served at the pleasure of the pastor and could be dismissed if they displeased him by complaining or protesting or exhibiting other inappropriate behavior. Indeed, a popular way of asserting authority once you put your feet under a table of your own was to fire everyone. Then it was *your* parish and that was that.

Some of the more recently ordained "John Paul II" clergy, believing as they do that their priestly identity depends on their authority, may restore this status quo, though there won't be any assistant pastors to dismiss. Until that counterrevolution becomes a fact, the parish staff—and often the turbulent staff meeting—will be a painful part of Catholic life. One hears stories of parishes breaking up because of conflict between the pastor and certain staff members or of new pastors being driven out because they were unable to reconcile factions within the parish.

Dr. Brown's portrait of the dynamics of the problem is insightful and challenging. Clearly, a major element of the conflicts is a pastor who lacks the maturity or the skills to preside over his staff. The ability to govern within collegiality should be a requirement for pastoral assignment, but it is not clear whether most dioceses have the kind of benches which provide replacements for the immature or unskilled.

Another dimension of the problem involves pastors who are well-meaning and want to be collegial in their governance who make one or two mistakes. They are not careful in screening the personalities of applicants for staff positions, and they lack the courage to terminate those who turn out to be disruptive. Priests tend by training and personality to want to help people and to give them one more chance—which often means that they are passively aggressive "nice guys." Yet to hire a blatantly troubled or angry person because the job might help the person does not help that person or other staff members or the parish. Not terminating an angry ideologue who is using the staff position as a base for fighting a cause will make a bad situation worse.

Choosing and presiding over a parish staff is a difficult and demanding task, especially since the contemporary minister is likely to be torn in many different directions by the conflicting—and often impossible—combination of demands that he experiences. If the staff is difficult, unstable and contentious, it ceases to be an essential support mechanism for his work. It becomes a decisive, not to say deadly dangerous, aspect of parish life.

When Ministry Is Messy is a major resource for priests and ministers who are trying to assemble functional staffs. It is evident that the wise and prudent pastor or minister must be sensitive and tough every step of the way.

Andrew Greeley
Mary Day in Harvest Time, 2005

INTRODUCTION

When I set out to write *When Ministry Is Messy: Practical Solutions to Difficult Problems*, I simply attempted to explore conflicts within Catholic ministry and possibly provide some practical solutions. What I soon discovered, thanks to Matthew 23, was the magnificent wisdom of Jesus, who put into practice many solutions to conflict with the religious ministers of his own time. The causes and solutions presented by Jesus give us a most special gift that provides new hope and peace for our ministry life.

I became interested in ministry conflict primarily because I was tired of seeing the best ministers quit or be fired. I also experienced my own versions of conflict. I suffered the loss of energy for my own ministry when another minister became jealous of my work. But, through the process of writing about this topic, I discovered a solution from Jesus' own example that ultimately became the whole purpose of this book. We, like Jesus who came into conflict with the religious leaders of his time in Matthew 23, must speak up. We must publicly and loudly name the sins that cause ministry conflict and provide solutions to those who will listen.

Two events spurred me on while writing about this topic. The first was that I found a gold mine of scriptural insight on ministry conflict. The second was that I recognized serious problems in my own ministry, as well as the Catholic ministry throughout the United States. But let us go first to the gold mine. I looked at the wisdom of modern psychology and common sense for the causes of conflict, and found that most conflicts could be reduced to three main causes: natural personality differences, emotional illness and sin.

Of course, one might argue that the primary solution to these major causes is one's ability to use logic or reason to overcome such inequities. But then I stumbled across Matthew 23 and I found a mother lode of God's wisdom on ministry conflict. It is in this chapter that we see Jesus in the temple courageously and loudly attacking the religious ministers of his time. He describes them, among other things, as "whitewashed tombs, which on the outside look beautiful, but inside...are full of the bones of the dead" (v. 27). In Chapter 23 I found all three of the main causes of ministry conflict, which I listed above, as well as three solutions to these difficulties that Jesus himself uses. And, not surprisingly, Jesus' solutions were perfect, logically and psychologically, for resolving all three of the conflict causes. I had struck gold.

But I also found problems during the process while conducting personal and phone interviews with diocesan-level leaders across the United States. I asked the following question: "What percentage of pastors, in your experience, has been emotionally ill enough that they have seriously harmed the ministries of their parish?" The responses to this question from these courageous leaders averaged a staggering 25 percent! The majority of responses fell within a range of 25–50 percent. Realizing the potential harm this could represent for ministry in America, I almost quit the project.

Those same diocesan heads, in responding to questions about the causes of and solutions to ministry conflict they had experienced, provided the following wisdom. Forty percent cited lack of communication or dialogue and lack of a shared vision as the core causes of ministry conflict. An additional 20 percent cited preoccupation with power or control. In the chapters ahead we will see that power issues and lack of dialogue result from natural personality differences, emotional illness and sin.

As to the most effective solutions to ministry conflict, the majority of diocesan leaders (54 percent) listed various forms of dialogue.

The other most-mentioned solutions were shared spirituality, ongoing formation of both lay and ordained ministers and third-party mediation. In identifying dialogue and communication as both the major problem and the major solution, there remains the issue as to how to initiate effective dialogue. The fundamental principle of this book is that ministry dialogue is only possible with the underlying attitudes, behavior and spirituality of loving servanthood, logic, loving forgiveness and courageous anger that Jesus models for us.

If you are involved in ministry, you most likely experience some sort of ministry conflict to a lesser or greater degree almost every day. You also might be aware that some of these conflicts are due, in large part, to natural personality differences. But the more serious issues that concern ministry life are those conflicts that arise because of emotional illness and sin. The more we explore these causes, the more we will understand and therefore better know what we can do about these potentially harmful situations. Jesus' three solutions provide us with a profound summary of a spirituality perfectly designed for ministers in handling conflict. Jesus' solutions—loving servanthood, logic, loving forgiveness and "speaking up"—provide us with a simple but profound summary of a spirituality perfectly designed for ministers in handling conflict.

AN OVERVIEW OF CONFLICT IN MINISTRY

Mary worked for years as the director of religious education for children in her parish. Thanks to her natural skills and generosity, she ran a successful program. Then her pastor fired her in a fit of irrational anger, following a difference of opinion that could have been worked out through communication. Later, the pastor admitted that his firing of Mary was a mistake. But Mary had already come very close to leaving ministry forever.

This is just one example of how conflict can harm God's ministry.

People in church ministry often bear the day-to-day realities of turf wars, character assassination, lying, power plays, derision, slander, alienation from fellow ministers, irrational anger, alcoholism, greed and pride. Other abuses include: jealousy, unfairness in the division of labor, limited emotional and financial support, degrading micromanagement, lack of training, procrastination, embezzlement and sexual and other types of harassment and intimidation.

Attacks and conflicts like these occur every day in Christian ministry, but they also occur between ministry leaders and the people to whom they minister. Whether the conflict and evil come from parents who complain about how their children are taught or from the children who cause trouble in the classroom, the causes and solutions remain the same no matter who does the harm to our ministry.

In answer to all of these attacks on God's ministers, what positive vision do you think God has for church ministry? Jesus said the purpose of life is to know and love God and to serve God through our loving service to others. Each ministry should somehow contribute to Jesus' purpose of drawing us into an ever-deepening relationship with God and each other. The day-to-day environment God intends for fruitful ministry includes love, helpfulness, generosity, support, appreciation, praise, encouragement, companionship, rationality, joy, humor and laughter—not conflict and evil.

• MINISTRY CONFLICT—THREE CAUSES AND POSSIBLE SOLUTIONS

To do something about the conflict and evil that prevents the full fruitfulness of God's ministries, we must focus on the three causes of ministry conflict: natural personality differences, emotional illness and sin. Understanding each of these causes and providing concrete solutions to control their impact will contribute to a powerful increase in fruitful ministries.

Natural Personality Differences

Natural personality differences are the most common causes of ministry conflict, and they are typically the easiest to spot and resolve. These differences occur because God made each of us with a unique set of psychological skills and talents. Later I will examine these skills in detail as well as explain how such a variety of skills, talents and personality traits can lead to clashes in the workplace and in ministry.

One example of how personality differences occur is when two people with very similar traits must work together. For example, Jack has a God-given skill in decision making, and, therefore, loves to be in charge. This skill brings him into conflict with another person to whom God has given the very same skill. A person like Jack, with this strong affinity to lead, can also conflict with someone who does not like to be told what to do, but rather prefers to be independent and do things his own way. All people face conflicts like this one every day, whether in ministry, their personal life or in the workplace. In order to survive, most people must overcome their personality differences and learn to get along for the sake of all. However, this might be easier said than done.

Here is another example that illustrates just how destructive personality conflicts can be within a parish and how difficult they can be to deal with: A liberal East Coast congregation received a pastor whom they perceived to be a conservative autocrat. Within the year of the pastor's arrival, the majority of the parish members did not agree with their new pastor's sermons, his ideology or his reconstruction of the ministries. Nevertheless, the pastor seemed unperturbed—he neither desired nor accepted any input from his parish members.

In response, the congregation's pastoral council appealed to the diocese for help. Instead of compromising or overcoming workable differences, the pastor and the congregation could not work together. The final result was a divisive one. Ultimately, the pastor asked his bishop to be removed from the parish and placed in a new pastorship. The bishop granted the request and the pastor left, taking a number of his more agreeable parishioners with him.

Possible Solutions to Natural Personality Differences
Natural personality differences are as varied as the conflicts they produce, and therein lay many solutions. Take for instance the case of the introvert and extrovert: A very sociable minister may feel that his emotional needs of communication and camaraderie are not being met by another in a ministry-related relationship. In turn, the less sociable or introverted minister may find it difficult to cope with the more gregarious minister who constantly wants to talk about seemingly unimportant matters. Both ministers often experience frustration and anger toward each other. Each feels like the other does not understand or respect him.

How would a situation like this be resolved? There are three effective strategies or solutions that can help overcome personality differences:

Recognition. The first step in overcoming differences is recognizing that they exist in the first place. If both parties recognize their personality differences, frustration can be prevented. And in the future, one might even try to overcome his or her natural predispositions and try to accommodate the other. This accommodation can come from intelligent, creative thinking—not to mention restraint in the case of the extrovert and a concerted effort in the case of the introvert. For example, the sociable minister can try to talk only about important matters to the nonsociable one, and the nonsociable minister likewise can go out of his way to talk about seemingly unimportant matters.

Acceptance. Another solution to differences in personality is for ministers to learn to accept differences and to celebrate them. Each different personality trait or talent represents a positive gift and contribution from God that can meet the many needs of ministry. There is room for everyone!

Prevention Through Communication. Another possible solution to personality conflicts is to prevent them from occurring in the first place. When every minister carefully understands, and in turn explains her own unique personality traits and needs to her fellow ministers, the likelihood of future conflict is greatly reduced. When others know where a minister is coming from or understand the minister's reasons for doing things a certain way (because she articulates these reasons effectively), they will be less likely to judge, misinterpret or become upset or offended by the minister's words or actions.

In chapter three we will describe in more depth the twelve most common personality traits that typically cause the most conflict, and how one might overcome such differences.

Emotional Illness

At first glance, emotional illness resembles sin and vice versa. A minister who behaves in a sinful manner, such as lying in order to have a fellow minister fired, may not intentionally sin or even be aware that he is indeed sinning, because of a highly anxious, emotionally unhealthy condition. Many times, jealousy and insecurity create great anxiety in ministry—and life in general. If that anxious fear blocks out one's ability to rationally control his behavior, one is less responsible for the seriousness of his sin. Nevertheless, the sin is still present and its impact is just as harmful to the victim.

Though emotional illness can vitiate the seriousness of the sin, we must maintain a strong concern about the impact of emotional illness in ministry leadership.

What are the signs of emotional illness in church ministry? Irrational behavior provides the most obvious sign. Does the ministry leader say or do things that make no sense? A single instance of irrational behavior can reflect human weakness. Oft-repeated occurrences can represent emotional instability or behavior that is uncontrolled by reason and common sense.

Irrational behavior that harms others, either emotionally or otherwise, poses a serious threat to ministry. A leader can become justifiably angry at a mistake of another leader that seriously disrupts the effectiveness of an event. But a leader who lashes out uncontrollably (for example, publicly deriding or demeaning a minister who may or may not have made a mistake) exhibits emotional illness. The irrationally angry minister destroys the emotional peace and self-esteem of other ministers by his words and erratic actions. Ultimately, these types of leaders interfere with and destroy the good works of the ministry itself.

Anxiety provides another sign of emotional illness. The emotionally healthy person certainly experiences moments of anxiety in ministry work, such as the moments before having to speak to the parishioners at a major ministry event.

But a fairly consistent state of anxiety in day-to-day living represents illness that God would prefer to have healed. Just look to what Jesus says in Matthew 6:25, "Therefore I tell you, do not worry about your life." Or in John 20:21 Jesus says, "Peace be with you."

Psychologists consider severe anxiety—a state of dread that has no rational basis known to the sufferer—as one of the most serious forms of human suffering. That person has a God-given right to professional relief. Meanwhile, that anxiety can produce its own harmful forms of "relief," such as irrational anger at the expense of other ministers.

Depression provides another visible sign of emotional illness. Depression is a highly complex disorder or disease that is not easily treated or understood. Many experts debate why depression develops, but most conclude that there are a variety of factors that lead to the onset of the disease, such as environmental and biological imbalances. Needless to say, depression makes a person unwell. And depression may also be the reason why one might experience sudden irrational outbursts of anger or rage that do not make sense or do not fit the situation.

Possible Solutions to Emotional Illness
Again there are three major means to effectively treat or prevent emotional illness from disrupting ministry work:

Prevention. The single most important way to resolve conflicts that arise from emotional illness in ministry is to prevent them from occurring in the first place. Parishes and dioceses must thoroughly research their prospective employees and ministers to determine if they are emotionally and psychologically stable for the work required of them. An example of how *not* to go about the hiring of ministers would be this all-too-familiar scenario: A bishop ignores the seminary-provided poor psychological profile of a prospective priest and hires him anyway because the diocese "needs the numbers."

When the emotional illness of the priest presents itself and he begins to harm others, the bishop covers up the indiscretions and moves the priest to another parish without notifying the new parish of the priest's condition.

A more positive and prevention-minded approach to the treatment of such a priest would be that the bishop heeded the warnings of the professional evaluation, pursued a professional second opinion and, if necessary, reported his findings and removed the priest from any potentially harmful situations. Prevention cannot be underestimated or overrated when hiring ministers.

Maintenance. The follow-up to prevention is maintenance. Once the ministers are hired by the diocese, members of the parish staff must all work together to maintain the health and well-being of ministers by providing effective outlets and resources to manage their mental and physical health. Maintaining the emotional health of ministers over the years requires placement in positions that match their unique skills and talents. For example, a minister should not be the primary administrator in a church when that minister only has a skill for providing physical and emotional care to those in need.

While these skills are a requisite to pastoral ministry, *leading* a parish requires other skills, such as administrative or business savvy as well as effective decision making. Also, ministers must be supported and given sufficient time for themselves, whether with family or other interests. Many other principles of maintaining emotional health remain, but the key is identifying the God-given gifts and needs of each person.

Identification. Needless to say, ministers are humans and humans are not perfect, and some emotional instability is likely to occur in reaction to life circumstances. The trick is to immediately identify and subsequently help heal those who become ill over the years. If the case is extremely serious, it will be necessary to fire those who become so unhealthy that they cannot change and become harmful to themselves or others. Unfortunately, the strong-willed and most determined personality—the most common in ministry leadership positions—can be the most reluctant to change in the counseling process.

Solutions to emotional illness also lie in spotting or identifying the slide from health to ill health over the years. We have discussed some of those identifiers already such as anxiety and irrational behavior in words or actions, including irrational outbursts of anger or the suppressed anger of depression.

Sin

Human sin, the third and less frequent cause of conflict and evil among ministers, is usually more hidden and more difficult to identify than natural personality differences or emotional illness. But sin, at its worst, is evil and may be the most destructive of human forces. Saint Thomas Aquinas, the primary doctor of Catholic theology, in his *Summa Theologica*, explores sins such as pride, greed, lying, calumny and lust, at great length. Each of these sins, according to Aquinas, occurs in every person's life and varies in degrees of seriousness, from the innocuous to the most destructive of evil.

Three traditional rules help identify sin as truly present and assess seriousness:
- Is the sin serious by its very nature?
- Is the sin committed with full awareness of its seriousness?
- Does the sinner freely and fully choose to do what is seriously harmful and evil?

Possible Solutions to Sin

Again, there are three effective ways in which a minister can overcome sin:

Prayer. As Catholics, we believe that prayer helps prevent sin. Therefore, praying for God's help in our ministry is most logical. Fasting also provides an effective means of calling on God's help.

Good Example. When we are not in the proper frame of mind or when we are so wrapped up in sinful behavior, it is good practice to look beyond the self toward others and follow their examples. For instance, one minister may unfairly deride another minister's work, even attempting to hide it under the guise of humor. Other ministers, however, can refuse to participate in that sinful game of hurting another and provide a positive environment instead.

Christian Admonition. The third solution to sin is that of verbal Christian admonition. In Matthew 18, Jesus describes this process: "If another member of the church sins against you, go and point out the fault when the two of you are alone....But if you are not listened to, take one or two others along with you, so that every word may be confirmed....If the member refuses to listen to them, tell it to the church" (vv. 15–17).

One of the most reported reasons for people leaving ministry is verbal abuse. This verbal abuse, which attacks a person's self-worth, is a sin against not only the individual ministry leader, but God's ministry itself. It is every minister's duty to set a proper example by dissuading any unhealthy or slanderous gossip, and by speaking out against those that participate in it.

QUESTIONS FOR DISCUSSION
1. What types of conflict have you experienced in ministry?
2. What were some of the causes?
3. What solutions worked for you?

CHAPTER TWO

JESUS' APPROACH TO CONFLICT IN MATTHEW 23

Before exploring the causes and solutions for ministry conflict and evil found in Matthew 23, let me first comment that I consider this chapter of the Bible as a profound gift from God. It is here that Jesus reveals to us that even the best and most esteemed members of society are capable of hypocrisy, scandal and sin. And it is in this chapter that we see the worst that ministry leadership can become. Jesus does not try to cover up these indiscretions. He hopes to expose them. Why? Jesus wants us all to understand that with authority and public esteem there are temptations to commit sins of pride, greed and sex, to name a few. Jesus wants us to be aware of these temptations because he himself was keenly aware of human behavior—and that even the best of humans are vulnerable to sin and conflict. Jesus wants us to understand this reality, because it is only after we understand it that we will be able to change it.

• DO WHATEVER THEY TEACH—NATURAL PERSONALITY DIFFERENCES
In Matthew 23, Jesus opens his attack on the Jewish religious leaders with recognition of their status. "The scribes and the Pharisees sit on Moses' seat; therefore, do whatever they teach you and follow it..." (v. 2). Jesus, however, is himself a religious leader and had been practicing his skills as a leader as far back as his teaching presence in the temple at the age of twelve. Jesus, therefore, is no stranger to what it takes to be a leader. Naturally, his preferred style of leadership clashes with that of the scribes and Pharisees.

So Jesus proceeds to challenge the leadership, having established the Pharisees as leaders (the term *scribe* may simply be another rendering of the term *Pharisee*), and clearly established himself as a religious leader. "…[B]ut do not do as they do, for they do not practice what they teach" (23:3). As we shall see later in sin as a cause of conflict and evil, Jesus even named this discrepancy between what they taught and what they did by saying, "[Y]ou…hypocrites!" (23:13).

These first fifteen verses continue with Jesus attacking their decisions as leaders, such as their prideful actions, doing "all their deeds to be seen by others" (23:5) and leading converts into their same sins. In verses 23–24, Jesus again refers back to their poor judgment as leaders, noting how they tithe mint and dill but "have neglected the weightier matters of the law: justice and mercy and faith."

Jesus clearly states in the first fifteen verses of this chapter his challenge of judgment and how to live as a religious leader representing God. The conflict between religious leaders flowing from natural personality differences is remarkably visible. In our time, most ministry leaders have their own stories to tell of these conflicts of judgment.

• WOE TO YOU, BLIND GUIDES!—EMOTIONAL ILLNESS

Jesus then provides an amazing picture of emotional illness in the psyche of the Pharisees. To place these verses in perspective requires that one recognizes that the primary way of detecting emotional illness is by observing irrationality in behavior. Irrationality can range from a simple case of anxiety to the extreme separation of intellect from imagination in a psychotic state, for example, hearing Jesus speak to us from the face of the moon. All kinds of human needs can generate the anxiety that produces irrational behavior, but sin can also be the human "need" that produces such behavior, such as in pride and greed.

Jesus begins by saying, "Woe to you, blind guides" (23:16). Emotional illness creates just such blindness. Emotions can blind our intellect and overwhelm our ability to stay rational. The worst emotional blindness in our personal relationship with God is that "hardness of heart" that Jesus notes in Mark 3:5–6: "He looked around at them [the Pharisees] with anger; he was grieved at their hardness of heart.…The Pharisees went out and immediately conspired with the Herodians against him, how to destroy him."

Having referred to the Pharisees' blindness, Jesus then gives full attention to their irrationality. He states that they say, "Whoever swears by the sanctuary is bound by nothing, but whoever swears by the gold of the sanctuary is bound by the oath" (23:16). In other words, they say that the gold has value and therefore can be sworn by. The sanctuary is of no account by comparison. But Jesus angrily argues, "You blind fools! For which is greater, the gold or the sanctuary that has made the gold sacred?" (23:17). He further expands on what he means by the word *sacred*: "whoever swears by the sanctuary, swears by it and by the one who dwells in it" (23:21).

So what emotion blinds the Pharisees from seeing that to swear by the sanctuary is to swear by the God who gives everything value? Greed. When the 400-plus Jewish synagogues brought in their offerings of gold to the temple, the Pharisees were the overseers as the heads of each of the synagogues. They were motivated by gold and money—not the sacred. In verse 25, Jesus will describe them as "full of greed." Greed can certainly blind the intellect and prevent logical, rational behavior. And again, in our time, many ministry leaders have their own stories to tell of blind irrationality, of the emotional illness other leaders have subjected them to.

• FULL OF GREED AND SELF-INDULGENCE—SIN
In Matthew Chapter 23 Jesus now describes the worst sins of religious leadership. "For you clean the outside of the cup and of the plate, but inside they are full of greed and self-indulgence" (25). Then he adds a similar image, that of the whitewashed tomb, "but inside they are full of the bones of the dead and all of kinds of filth" (v. 27). And again, "inside you are full of hypocrisy and lawlessness" (v. 28). So in the midst of saying how full of sin these religious leaders are, Jesus again

rightfully uses the term hypocrisy. Three times, in verses 25, 27 and 29, he begins his list of their sins by saying, "Woe to you, scribes and Pharisees, hypocrites!" What could be more hypocritical than a religious leader who represents God and teaches the way to God externally, but who internally rejects God through sin?

A final description of their sin follows Jesus' third "hypocrites!" outburst. He comes to the greatest of their sins, that of murder. He starts with their own professed denial of following in the footsteps of their ancestors in the killing of the prophets. Instead, Jesus knows that they will "kill and crucify" and "flog in your synagogues" the prophets God sends, and the blood of all the generations of prophets will come down upon these present Pharisees (vv. 34–35). Jesus will become the object of their greatest sin, their greatest evil as ministry leaders.

The final three verses of Chapter 23 will provide us later with a transition from this worst of the Pharisees' sins, killing the prophet, to God's most powerful action, loving forgiveness.

• THE GREATEST...WILL BE YOUR SERVANT—LOVING SERVANTHOOD
We now proceed to the solutions to conflict and evil that God presents to us in Matthew. As we shall see, each of the three solutions Jesus uses is effective for all three of the above causes of conflict and evil. The resolving power of servanthood begins our list of solutions.

In the midst of attacking the Pharisees for their sinful ways as ministry leaders, Jesus recommends a brilliant, logical solution to the most typical of ministry sins, pride. "The greatest among you will be your servant" (23:11). Jesus' mother, Mary, had put this servanthood into practice at the Annunciation, saying to the angel Gabriel, "Here am I, the servant of the Lord; let it be with me according to your word" (Luke 1:38). Ministry servanthood begins with our servant relationship with God. We accept God as our whole focus in all our work. We take on the attitude of doing what God needs and judges. As Jesus stated in a prior verse, "And call no one your father on earth, for you have one Father—the one in heaven" (Matthew 23:9). Servanthood reaches out to all whom we deal with in ministry, including our fellow ministers.

Servanthood works best for the first mentioned cause of ministry conflict—natural personality differences. The primary form of this conflict is the natural conflict in decision making. Each leader wants to direct the way things go. But in servanthood, the first leader takes on the attitude of listening to the needs and judgments of the second leader. The second leader responds with the same attitude toward the needs and judgment of the first leader. Thus we have two leaders who do not fail to listen to each other. From this discussion flows a willingness to look at all the facts, compromise, resolve conflict and avoid evil.

As to the second cause of ministry conflict and evil—emotional illness—Jesus' solution of servanthood also heals. Anxiety reigns as the primary internal experience of emotional illness. But if one approaches the ill person with an attitude of servanthood, friendly openness to where the emotionally troubled person is at and what his or her needs are, chances are the ill person's anxiety will be relieved.

Servanthood also can be used to conquer sin. One may be sinfully proud in her position as a representative of God, seeing herself as the only source of all her value. But a person who possesses an attitude of servanthood toward both God and other people directly contradicts and washes out such pride.

In other sins, one can freely choose to ignore the truth and do what one knows God does not want. Taking on the attitude and behaviors of a servant reminds one of the truth. As a ministry leader, an attitude of servitude directs all toward God's humble, loving judgment to where one's true needs and true happiness lie.

• FOR WHICH IS GREATER—LOGIC

The use of logic provides a natural, powerful tool in solving all three of the causes of ministry conflict and evil. We see Jesus use logic throughout Matthew 23, whether in dealing with his conflict with the Pharisees when he attacks their judgment as leaders or in trying to break through their emotional illness and their sins.

Logic is a function of the intellect. The way to force the intellect (logic) to function is to ask questions. So throughout his attacks on the leadership judgments of the Pharisee leaders, Jesus asks questions, such as, "For which is greater, the gift or the altar that makes the gift sacred?" (v. 19). His questions are intended to force their intellects to find the truth.

Jesus also uses logic in dealing with the Pharisees' emotional ill health. The whole series of his questioning their irrational, illogical approach to what one swears by in the temple represents an attempt to break through their emotional blindness. We have noted greed as a possible emotion that blinds them. Pride may also be blinding them, as a fancy new car can cause a person to believe that is what gives them his value as a person.

The valuable gifts and gold that accrue to the synagogues and the temple could represent to the leaders their own personal value. In modern day counseling, logic and factual truth are at the center of healing. Logic can finally break through the irrationality and the emotional blindness that produces the anxiety.

In dealing with the Pharisees' serious sin of contemplating Jesus' death, Jesus again uses a question to force logic as a solution to break through their hard hearts. "How can you escape being sentenced to hell?" (23:33). In other words, the logic of their sin is that it will result in hell. One of the ways of dealing with any sin is to consider, through questioning, "What are the logical consequences of this sin?"

• AS A HEN GATHERS HER BROOD—LOVING FORGIVENESS

After listing the Pharisees' sins as religious leaders, Jesus then provides an alternative—loving forgiveness. This not only resolves the problem of their sins, but also has the power to resolve the problems of the other two causes: natural personality differences and emotional illness.

In Matthew 23 Jesus cries out: "Jerusalem, Jerusalem, the city that kills the prophets and stones those who are sent to it!"(v. 37). He thus makes a direct reference to the greatest of their sins to come—the killing of him. He wants to help them avoid this most serious sin. He proceeds with his impressive mother-hen solution of tenderness, compassion and loving forgiveness. "How often have I desired to gather your children together as a hen gathers her brood under her wings, and you were not willing!" (23:37). Conjoined with the just-mentioned "Jerusalem, Jerusalem…" opening regarding their desire to kill him, this mother-hen image carries a message of forgiveness. God humbly, lovingly reaches out to the Pharisees in their sin, inviting them into a forgiving embrace. With the last phrase, "you were not willing," Jesus, however, both names their behavior as conscious sin and emphasizes to the Pharisees that he is talking about them.

We need to point out here that the forgiveness of Jesus, of God, comes logically from one who loves. All forgiveness is based on our love for the other person. God so loves us that God forgives us, as long as we are willing to accept the forgiveness.

Now we should explore how this loving forgiveness of God logically and psychologically resolves the three causes of ministry conflict and evil. Taking them in order, how does loving forgiveness heal natural personality differences? You and I as leaders may angrily conflict over a ministry decision, or you may be sociable and I am not, therefore we cause each other pain. But your loving forgiveness of my hurting you will resolve the situation. And I will return the favor by forgiving you, by bringing you under my wings.

Loving forgiveness heals emotional illness and is a logical antidote to the low self-esteem, poor self-image and feelings of unworthiness that are often at the heart of anxiety and fear. *I know how my anxiety-produced irrational anger has harmed you, and yet you value and love me enough to forgive me.* In other words, "Forgive me, because you love me, because you think that I am worthwhile!"

As the solution to sin, loving forgiveness provides the chance for the sinner to abandon his sin, and to embrace instead his greatest need, that of a true, personal love. Jesus says to the Pharisees, in effect, "I lovingly forgive you for wanting to kill me." This has the greatest chance of breaking the hard-heartedness of their sinful state. However, when a person's sin is mingled with emotional illness, such as an emotionally blinding pride, it is very difficult to reach or change this person. The Pharisees, for example, could not and would not accept Jesus' loving forgiveness, not just because of their own sins, but because of their own displaced emotional state.

• The City That Kills the Prophets—Choosing to "Stay Stuck" in Conflict

In spite of the three effective alternatives Jesus affords the Pharisees, the Pharisees still choose to "stay stuck" in conflict and evil. Jesus sums it up perfectly in Matthew 23 when he says, "you were not willing"(v. 37). The Pharisees choose to "stay stuck" and ultimately kill their prophet just to shut him up.

In our ministry today, we experience many versions of the same thing—although not to the same degree. Nevertheless, a leader may "kill" or, more aptly, get rid of another minister by firing him. A leader or general minister may kill by socially isolating another from staff and parishioners. Leaders or other ministers may also spread lies about another minister's behavior, or repeat any truthful negatives they can discover, so they may denigrate the fellow minister. Some ministers may aim to take away the power of their leader. Many ministers, despite knowing what they are doing is wrong and destructive, want to remain in their anxiety, their fear, their jealousy, their greed, their struggle for their own prideful power.

But again in Chapter 23, Jesus provides a way to get beyond this hurtful behavior. Jesus calls for an unlikely solution—courageous anger. Jesus repeats this line six times in Matthew 23: "But woe to you, scribes and Pharisees, hypocrites!" (v. 13). Also, we hear his angry voice say, "Woe to you, blind guides" (v. 16), "You blind fools!" (v. 17), "You blind Pharisee!" (v. 26), "You snakes, you brood of vipers!" (v. 33). Jesus speaks up with courageous force, naming the emotional illness of blindness, and the sin, the two hardest causes of conflict and evil to resolve.

We may face a leader whose personality difference with us becomes an emotional illness causing him to sin against us. Like Jesus, we in turn need to strongly speak up against the evil directed at others or ourselves. Speaking up takes courage in the face of possible consequences, but the anger of Jesus took courage as he attempted to challenge the religious leaders of his time in their illness and sin.

Jesus lost after he had done all he could to break the conflict and evil of the Pharisees. They later lied about him, calling Jesus an imposter (27:63). They saw to his killing. So, as it was with Jesus, perhaps the reaction to one's efforts to resolve conflict and evil may include "apparent" total failure. But the fruits of our efforts may show later on. Our servanthood, logic, loving forgiveness or courageous anger may finally have an effect and produce peaceful resolution. Meanwhile, we can rest at peace with our God in knowing we have practiced what Jesus practiced in dealing with conflict and evil.

QUESTIONS FOR DISCUSSION

1. As a religious minister, what most strikes you as you read Matthew, Chapter 23?
2. What warnings about behaviors and attitudes do you find for the religious ministers of our day in Jesus' warnings to the religious ministers of his day?
3. What solutions did Jesus use to solve the concerns he had?

CHAPTER THREE

NATURAL PERSONALITY DIFFERENCES

The majority of conflict and evil in ministry results from natural personality differences. As we have just seen, Jesus struggled with his leadership skills to change the Pharisee leaders. Jesus' own mother conflicted with him over his ministry decisions. When he was a youth at the temple, talking with the religious leaders, Mary questioned his having stayed behind (Luke 2:48–50). At Cana, she challenged his initial refusal to perform the miracle of the wine that would begin his public ministry (John 2:3–5). The Gospels thus reflect the reality of day-to-day leadership conflict coming from natural skill or personality differences.

So to solve conflict we must understand this primary cause. I have explored this issue, both in psychology and in Scripture, since the mid-70s when I titled my doctoral research, *An Exploration of Teacher-Student Relationships*. No issue in ministry has more daily practical relevance than how we deal with relationship conflict, irritation, concern, anger—evil that is happening to us in ministry leadership. A positive resolution most often flows from understanding the cause and thereby coming up with an intelligent solution.

• THE VALUE OF IDENTIFYING PERSONALITY SKILLS

Besides the value of understanding the primary reason conflict happens, we will also identify other personality skill values, as we (1) explore God's overall plan for human life, (2) seek God's will for our unique individual life, (3) learn how to achieve happiness, (4) acquire emotional health, and (5) enhance human motivation and productivity in ministry.

God's wisdom for all of these values or benefits comes again from Scripture, Matthew 25:14–30, the parable of the talents. Near the end of his life, as in his attack on the Pharisees in Matthew 23, Jesus provides a summary of help for future ministry. In this parable he outlines the overall plan of God's kingdom on earth in preparing for eternal life. The Master entrusts three different combinations of "talents" to his three servants. Then he leaves them, expecting the best use of what he has given. When he returns, two have traded their talents. The fearful third servant has buried his talent. He is sent by the master to "the outer darkness, where there will be weeping and gnashing of teeth" (Matthew 25:30).

1. Explore God's overall plan for human life.

These "talents" in Jesus' parable are provable as the unique combinations of natural psychological skills with which God endows each of us. We are expected to use them in service to others, in effect trading them with others who use their unique set of skills in service to us. In our life of unique service, we thereby end life with a multiplicity of talents received in the process of bartering talents with others. By "trading" we help merit God's invitation to "enter into the joy of your master" (Matthew 25:23).

One may wonder why God gives a different set of personality skills to each person, which then in turn becomes such a major cause of conflict between people. The parable of the talents again provides the wisdom. Since we each have different skills, we must help one another, trading what we can do with what the other person can do. We are, in effect, forced to act out in service our love for each other, the active love that God intends as our primary way of salvation.

2. Seek God's will for our unique individual life.

Not only does this parable tell us God's general plan for our life, but we also can learn his particular will for our own life. We do not have to sit back and wait for God's voice to tell us what God wills for our particular journey. We do need to pray always for God's light and strength of discernment. But all we need to do is intelligently notice what we most enjoy doing and are most good at. Doing so will guide us to recognize our natural personality skills or talents. This in turn tells us the activities God wants us to do with most of our day-to-day life, such as our career, marriage and free time. I will expand on this in detail in the next section of this chapter.

3. Learn how to achieve happiness.

Another value of identifying our skills lies in the happiness that comes from *using* our skills. To use our skills, to match them to what we spend our life doing and to those we spend our life with, creates the greatest natural source of happiness available. God made the human personality open to happiness also, if we would just listen to how we are made.

4. Acquire emotional health.

Emotional health is closely aligned with how we experience happiness and peace. To the extent we listen to and use our unique skills, we normally eliminate anxiety, the primary symptom of emotional illness. So, if we enjoy and become proficient in math and use math in service to others, each such event helps to ensure our overall emotional health. I use the term *normally* because chemically caused anxiety exists, due to abnormalities that can occur in the brain. Providentially, scientists in our own time are learning to correct this imbalance. For ministry, our emotional health keeps us from contributing to the second cause of conflict and evil, emotional illness.

5. Enhance human motivation and productivity in ministry.

Another value of identifying natural personality skills comes from the powerful motivation and productivity that flows from the happiness and emotional health we have just described. If our primary unique skills match what our ministry needs, we are highly motivated by the enjoyment that using our skills produces. High motivation in turn makes for high productivity and successful ministry.

First, we will identify how these different natural personality skills cause conflict. If you know your skills and can recognize other people's skills, you have what it takes to understand most conflicts going on between you and them. After that, the solutions are just common sense.

• IDENTIFYING PERSONALITY SKILLS

What are the natural personality skills with which God endows us? Psychologists have provided us with many different attempts to list them. As I searched for years for common denominators, the best grouping I could find was that of Edwin Megargee. I used his *California Psychological Inventory,* with its 400-plus questions, for evaluating the skills of Christian leaders across the United States. I found that when the leaders identified their strongest skills, they took much better advantage of them in their ministry. For over twenty years I worked at coming up with a shorter skills list that everyone could identify with and easily apply in ministry.

In the following list, pick out the skills you most enjoy using.* Also, pick out the ones you least enjoy. This helps round out the picture of your unique God-given personality skills. The twelve skills are:

1. Decision making
People who possess this skill enjoy leading others. They are the decision makers and like to take charge. They enjoy giving advice and direction.

2. Sociability
The talkative tend to possess this skill. These people enjoy and are con-

---

* A more comprehensive description of these twelve natural personality skills is available in the form of a self-scoring questionnaire, in chapter four of my book, *A Practical Guide for Starting an Adult Faith Formation Program* (San Jose: Resource Publications, 2003).

fident in group situations. Light conversation with a stranger at "the drop of a hat" delights them.

3. Organization
People with this skill like order. Everything is kept in its proper place, whether it is files or the day's schedule. Those who possess this skill avoid impulsive behavior.

4. Responsibility
Those who possess this skill enjoy carrying out a task to its completion. They are conscientious, dependable and govern their lives by reason.

5. Logical intelligence
People with this skill prefer step-by-step logic to solve a problem. They can accept the value of rules and regulations.

6. Intuitive intelligence
People with this skill excel in original thought and creativity. They come up with new ideas, solutions and directions. Authoritarianism repels them.

7. Artistic intelligence
Those who have this skill enjoy creating or simply appreciating beauty, such as painting, music and dance. Sunsets, mountain views and beautiful people excite them.

8. Counsel
Good counselors perceive people's feelings, needs and concerns, even when the others have not stated how they feel. This skill draws people to seek their help.

9. Nurturance
People who possess this skill are responsive to the physical and emotional needs of others. They like to verbalize feelings and be physically affectionate. Hospitality reigns.

10. Flexibility

People who possess this skill judge each situation on its own merit, rather than limit themselves to a few set principles in life. They are flexible rather than rigid or dogmatic.

11. Tolerance

People who possess this skill are open to personalities different from their own. They accept without judgment others' beliefs and attitudes. They are trusting and nonauthoritarian.

12. Emotional Health

People who are emotionally healthy are peaceful rather than anxious and enjoy a rational, positive outlook. They look forward to the day enjoying what they do well.

One's ability to identify these twelve major personality traits in other people will contribute most to resolving day-to-day ministry conflicts and evil. This ability of identification lies simply in noticing what others enjoy and what they do not enjoy doing. Also, given time and opportunity to develop, what they enjoy should also become what they are good at. That enjoyment conveys the unique skills with which God endowed them. Watch others' behavior for clues and listen closely to what they say. Listen for, "I really like to…" or "I really hate to…." These are the "life enjoyment" questions to ask when interviewing a candidate for ministry work. Though not directly related to ministry itself, they are no less important when trying to discover where a person's interests and skills lie.

Understanding natural personality skills is about connecting the psychological experience of enjoyment that flows from having a skill to the fact that you also have a need for that enjoyment. For example, you have the skill of an animal to eat to maintain your physical nature. You also have a need to eat, a need to use that skill. In your human personality, you may have a strong nurturing skill, but this automatically gives you a strong need to be nurturing whenever you get the chance. As we shall see, when that need is denied or cannot function, anger and conflict result.

We will now consider how anger comes from the denial of our needs. God put anger in our personality as a way to ensure that we meet our legitimate needs. God cannot miraculously step in and take care of each of them for us, no matter how much God loves us. Besides depending on others to respond to our needs, as we saw in the parable of the talents, God has built into us various tools by which we see to our own needs. The natural response of anger when our needs are not being met provides one of the most effective of those tools. When we cannot use a skill, anger provides us with the energy to see that we get the chance to use our denied natural personality skill.

• How Natural Personality Skills Cause Conflict

We naturally move from the dynamics of anger to how natural personality skill differences cause conflict. When ministry leaders have different skills, and therefore differing needs, the potential for not meeting each other's needs is huge. Needs that are not met lead to anger, and anger often leads to conflict. This simple formula for conflict represents why so much relationship conflict exists in ministry.

Another element we need to mention is the fact that every person has all of the psychological skills. Comparing a full glass of water to a glass with only a quarter inch of water, we see that both contain water. So also each person has at least a minimum of each skill. The differences in levels of skill make one person strong in some areas, while another person is strong in others. But each strong set of skills represents a different set of strong needs. People therefore come in conflict when they do not meet each other's needs due to different skills.

A very sociable minister may feel irritated, even angered, by a reclusive new minister. The new minister in turn feels angered by the constant attempts of the very sociable one to break through his chosen wall, and so avoids the encounters at all costs. Unique personality skill differences produce unmet needs. Anger and conflict reign.

The one exception to this rule is in the skill of decision making. If there are two ministers who are the same, this causes the conflict of both wanting to be in charge. For example, Joan, a natural leader, may feel her fiefdom in church ministry is threatened by the arrival of a new minister who has similar interests. Joan's need for control is at risk. Her resulting anger leads her to enforce her authority in the area of ministry by looking for faults in the new minister.

The tantrum of a two-year-old child provides us with strong early evidence in human nature of the connection of anger to differences in natural personality skills. Ask any parent to describe the positive personality characteristics of his or her child, and to then carefully notice what precedes the angry tantrum. A very bright and emotionally healthy child cannot yet verbalize his or her needs well at this age, and so important personality needs are not met. Usually, that is the source of the anger. For example, a very independent child may on occasion say, "I do!" But the parent recognizes that just before a tantrum, the child was trying to accomplish something and the parent tried to help out. Suddenly the tantrum comes when the need to be independent is frustrated, and the child cannot remember what to say.

The ministry leader may experience similar anger when his or her natural personality skills, and therefore his or her strong needs, are frustrated.

• TWELVE SKILLS AND HOW THEY CAUSE CONFLICT

After talking about natural personality skills and how preventing their functioning causes anger, we now look at how each of these skills causes conflict. The purpose of this section is to review the twelve skills above and to find the ones that are the strongest in yourself or another minister. Here we have simple relationship descriptions of (a) why a person strong in skills feels irritated or angry, and (b) why the other person in the relationship, who is low in the same skills (except in decision making), feels irritated or angry. Each explanation is followed by an example of such conflict types. The twelve conflict descriptions are:

1. Decision making

(a) The person strong in this skill hates it when others challenge her judgment. She thinks that others ignore her requests and try to take over.

(b) The person who has this same strong skill is frustrated by the other person's not listening to his judgment. He thinks that she wants her way all the time.

Example: Jane was hired as pastoral administrator a year ago. Her leadership style is to give ministry leaders as much freedom as possible, to support their decisions. But Henry, in charge of youth ministry, constantly gives orders to maintenance people without consulting with Jane who has made clear that it is her responsibility.

2. Sociability

(a) The person who possesses this skill feels anger when people ignore or reject his friendliness. Loneliness or social depression sets in when socializing is at a minimum.

(b) A person low in this skill dislikes talkative people and prefers time alone. She also feels anxiety in group situations. And given the opportunity, she prefers serious talk over small talk.

Example: John heads his local Knights of Columbus group. Meeting once a month and also doing group service activities meets most of the men's needs. But one of the Knights, Richard, keeps insisting with John that there is too much random talk going on at the meetings. Richard insists on being the sergeant-at-arms.

3. Organization

(a) The person who is highly organized gets angry when things are not where they should be. People who are off-schedule irritate him or her, and that irritation is visible when another forgets something, is not prompt or is unkempt.

(b) The person who does not possess a strong version of this skill becomes angry when the "organizer" gets upset with his or her lack of organization. In order to show his or her anger or displeasure at the organizer, he or she becomes even more disorganized.

Example: The church youth group has a separate Bible study component on every Wednesday night. Mary likes to plan the topics of all the meetings a year ahead of schedule. Recently, the pastor required her to open up each week's decision to the group as to what Scripture would be discussed the following week.

4. Responsibility

(a) In this conflict situation, the person strong in this skill gets angry when a fellow minister does not get his or her job done on time. He or she hates chaos.

(b) The person who is low in this skill hates being reminded he or she is off-schedule. He or she sees living with chaos as a challenge to his or her survival skills.

Example: The marriage prep ministry provides a quarterly all-day seminar for engaged couples new to their program. The team of five couples who run the program divides up the all-day seminar responsibilities. In a final check the day before, the team learns one couple forgot to rent the space or order the food.

5. Logical intelligence

(a) The person with this skill is irritated by those who make seemingly irrational or snap decisions. Irrationality angers him or her.

(b) A person with little logical intelligence considers the step-by-step logic for decision making an irritating waste of time. He or she angrily pushes to move on to the next agenda item.

Example: Elementary education at the church in question suffers a great loss of enrollment, because Pastor Albert has suggested that the parents had to attend a family-based program, not just drop off their children. At a staff meeting, George quickly reacts to the pastor's decision by shouting out, "Go back to drop-off!"

6. Intuitive intelligence

(a) A person with this skill hates to have his or her spontaneous insight or solution to a problem dismissed "out-of-hand." To have to explain the logic irritates this person.

(b) On the other hand, a person low in this skill hates quick solutions. He or she laughs at the potential absurdity of these solutions. Intuition irritates him or her.

Example: Bible study, as a part of Saint Thomas the Apostle adult education program, gives Joan weekly opportunities to provide spontaneous insights. But Elizabeth objects almost every time, trying to show how it does not make sense. Some support Joan. Others support Elizabeth.

7. Artistic intelligence

(a) People with artistic intelligence become depressed when they are not able to express themselves artistically. They hate having someone cut off their enjoyment of a sunset.

(b) For a person without this skill, hours spent on liturgical decorations are a waste of time. Invitations to an opera, symphony, museum tour or ballet are turned down.

Example: As the head of liturgical ministry, James has planned months in advance the coming Christmas celebration. He will play special organ music, along with his 80-voice choir. At their last and critical rehearsal, the maintenance man suddenly shows up demanding to shampoo the carpeting.

8. Counsel

(a) People who are not forthright about their feelings irritate the person with this skill. It irritates or angers them when others deny their perceptions.

(b) A person without this skill resists and is angered by efforts to encourage him or her to be emotionally intimate. A person adverse to closeness avoids the open interchange of feelings.

Example: Mary Ann immediately noticed the high level of anger of both husband and wife as they entered her counseling ministry office. After the opening pleasantries, the couple denied they felt any anger. After forty-five minutes of each trying to control the conversation, they both admitted to hating each other for that behavior.

9. Nurturance

(a) A person with this skill hates it when others refuse his or her efforts to take care of them, such as cooking a meal or other physical or emotional support.

(b) Physical displays of affection, like hugs, irritate a person without this skill. He or she feels trapped by another person who is always trying to take care of him or her.

Example: Helping to prepare and serve food to the poor each day for the outreach ministry was the highlight of the pastor's day. However, when Bob went to the bishop on his annual visit, the bishop insisted the two hours a day was a misuse of the pastor's time. In spite of his anger, the pastor did more of the hated paperwork.

10. Flexibility

(a) A person with this skill is angered by inflexible rules or principles that allow no exceptions. Statements like "all women are that way" or "he will never change" irritates him or her.

(b) A person without this skill fears life's instability, so he or she follows a few simple principles by which he or she judges everything. He or she hates the more complicated views of situations.

Example: Alice is amazed at all the complications involved in the fundraising ministry she has just joined. For example, how do you deal with people when you ask them face-to-face to tithe? Adam insists the only thing that works is to tell the story of your own tithing. Alice insists there must be many other possibilities.

11. Tolerance

(a) People's lack of tolerance and acceptance of anyone "different" makes a person with this skill uncomfortable and irritated. They hate sexism, racism and other "isms."

(b) Fear converts to anger for persons who lack much tolerance. They are irritated by others who do not understand their fear.

Example: In charge of youth ministry, Maria, a Hispanic woman, was greatly admired for her handling of the mixed Hispanic-Caucasian youth. She actively taught and showed tolerance. But suddenly a white parent loudly proclaimed his daughter was being harassed by some of the Hispanic young people. His daughter turned out to be the culprit.

12. Emotional health

(a) The anxiety of others makes a person with this skill irritated or uncomfortable. He or she resists that which would irrationally try to take away their peace. They resist with logic.

(b) Those with anxiety are irritated by the self-confidence and rationality of the peaceful ones. They anxiously live in a world of fear, anger and depression.

Example: Sylvester wanted to start up a new divorced singles group for his church. He felt there were parishioners often experiencing loneliness and anxiety. Confident he could be of service, he asked the pastor's permission. The pastor said no, citing his fear of alienating married couples.

QUESTIONS FOR DISCUSSION

1. What experiences have you had with natural personality differences between yourself and another minister?

2. What differences have been the most common as you have observed the personality conflicts among other ministers?

3. Which of your personal experiences in this cause of conflict made you the angriest?

EMOTIONAL ILLNESS

We will now explore further, (1) behaviors related to emotional illness in church ministry, (2) the impact of that behavior on victims, (3) how emotionally ill behaviors seriously damage ministries, (4) the need to not overreact to single instances of apparent emotional illness behavior, (5) the insufficient reactions by observers of the emotionally ill, and (6) how the emotionally ill bypass evaluations in seminaries, parish hiring and interviews of volunteers.

• THE BEHAVIORS OF EMOTIONAL ILLNESS

The primary characteristics or visible signs of emotional illness include anxiety, depression and irrationality. From these conditions, many behaviors follow.

Anger in itself is a God-given, natural response to what is legitimately bad for us or others. This emotional response gives us the energy to eliminate the bad. We can thus can defend ourselves and be an instrument of love as Jesus has commanded us to be. But the irrational anger of the emotionally ill is not what God intends. For example, the firing of a successful staff member, in a pastor's fit of irrational anger, destroys ministry.

Irrational anger is behavior that does not make sense. The victim may say, "Why are you doing this? The punishment just doesn't fit what my behavior has actually been. I've been successful in my ministry. I'm a good person with human flaws, but not flaws that would logically result in being fired and all the evil this will cause for me and for my ministry."

Judging whether anger is irrational or justified depends on the use of the human intellect in judging what is true and therefore rational. We need to trust our God-given intellect to come up with the truth. The way we get the intellect to function in order to produce that truth is simply to ask a question: "Why is someone reacting like this?" This question requires the intellect to come up with a truthful, rational answer. If no answer surfaces that justifies a particular firing, the truth is that there *is* no rational reason. However, there may be a just reason for the firing, and that is why the question is asked—to get at the facts. Mary asked the young Jesus in the temple after he was missing for three days, "Child, why have you treated us like this?" His response was legitimate, but difficult to understand: "Did you not know that I must be in my Father's house?" (Luke 2:48, 49). In the case of the angry pastor, if the firing seems irrational and the pastor provides no just reason, one might conclude that his behavior and subsequent firing of the minister may be due to emotional illness.

We must also note that irrational behavior does not always represent an underlying emotional illness. For example, a diocesan e-mail announcing a new series of training seminars for catechists may not include a seminar you had been told to give and had already fully prepared. You start going up the chain of authority to find out why you were excluded from the e-mail. Some initial possibilities for the apparently irrational behavior could range from incompetence to jealousy to emotional illness. After getting whatever facts you can, the judgment of emotional illness may only result in unwarranted suspicion. More incidents are normally required to provide a diagnosis and thus what actions one must take to address the situation. The seriousness of even one incident, however, may require that one act.

Besides anxiety, which can produce irrational anger, depression is another sign. One way in which the complex disease of depression can begin is with the typical substratum of emotional illness and a general lack of self-worth. The pattern producing this type of depression goes as follows: *I do not value my right to be angry and speak up to achieve my legitimate, rational needs. So I suppress my anger.* The covered-over, suppressed anger looks like a significant state of having no feelings, or a state of depression. This state can easily include not speaking up for my needs, which therefore do not get attended to. This creates anger, which again gets suppressed and only increases the depression and often leads to apparent sadness. "Poor me" is one of the expressions we may hear. The low self-worth, sadness, lack of energy, guilt and other related symptoms help us identify this depressed condition as emotional illness.

Irrationality is our third condition or sign of emotional illness. We have seen irrationality in the form of irrational anger produced by anxiety. We have also discussed how the intellect lets us know whether the observed behavior is irrational or rational. But irrationality can be seen in other behaviors besides irrational anger.

• The Impact of Emotional Illness Behaviors on Victims

We discerned three signs of emotional illness as anxiety, depression, irrationality and their resulting behaviors. Now we will see that the victims of those behaviors, in turn, can come to suffer similar conditions or signs even though they are not emotionally ill. They can experience their own feelings of anxiety, depression and irrationality as a direct, logical result of being victimized by the emotionally ill.

For example, if I have to work with a minister who is often very anxious, then I as a victim of that behavior may observe myself as more anxious. If that ill person is regularly seriously depressed, I may find myself becoming depressed. If he or she often flares up in irrational anger, I may catch myself constantly worrying about what may come next. The anxious, depressed or irrational climate produced by the emotionally ill minister can directly harm the levels of peace, positive attitude and rationality of fellow ministers.

• THE IMPACT OF EMOTIONAL ILLNESS BEHAVIORS ON MINISTRIES

Since we are involved in serving both people and God in religious ministry work, an additional concern is the impact of illness behaviors on the ministries themselves. Do these behaviors destroy God's ministries?

If a capable, effective leader of a successful parish's ministry is fired because of the emotionally ill, irrational behavior of a pastor, then the ministry's effectiveness can be destroyed. The unreasonable firing of good personnel is a major typical behavior that harms all the future potential work of the ministry. These firings can happen both at the parish and the diocesan level. Some of the human values wiped out by an irrational firing are the years of fruitful relationships established, the group vision developed and the trust and confidence won. All the graces that flow through such human bonds are frustrated until an equally qualified leader can rebuild the ministry. Meanwhile, there can be years of less qualified leadership inhibiting the ministry's potential fruitfulness.

Besides the harm of irrational firing, the fruitfulness of ministries can also be destroyed by the anxiety, depression and irrationality of the individual leader of a ministry. If your leader is anxious, depressed or irrational, who wants to follow? You may then leave that ministry as a volunteer or as a participant. And who wants to be served by such a minister? For example, if you are homebound and receive Communion through an irritable and confusing eucharistic minister, you may try to get another minister or simply give up the service.

A third impact by an emotionally ill leader is the destruction of the strength and motivation of a fellow minister. It could be a question of the strong, demeaning nature of the emotionally ill person's attack on others. The irrational rage could undermine the other minister's self-esteem, which in turn would affect the motivational strength of that person's leadership. The lack of motivation and purpose on the part of the leader would then cause the ministry to not function well.

Procrastination is another typical result of low self-esteem induced by personal, irrational attacks by a superior or a co-minister.

• THE NEED TO AVOID OVERREACTION TO SINGLE INSTANCES

We are obligated to act in response to the seriously anxious, depressed or irrational behaviors of the emotionally ill, both for the sake of their ministry and for their sake as human persons. But there is a major caveat. You may have spotted an instance in your own behavior of being seriously anxious, depressed or irrational. Or you may have spotted an instance in the behavior of a fellow minister. You could then ask yourself such questions as:

1) Was the behavior serious in its impact on others or myself?
2) Has this behavior or similarly anxious, depressed or irrational behaviors happened more than once?

If your response is "no" to both questions, you most likely would not consider the behavior as coming from serious emotional illness that requires your action.

Taking an example from family life, a mother may recall that last week she reacted with a serious outburst of anger to the behaviors of her two children who had been testing her right to control their behavior. In looking back, she may judge that her outburst of anger was irrational in its verbal content. But under the circumstances of their behavior, she can see that there was a solid case to be made for her anger, even if it ended up in an outburst. For the emotionally ill, one would usually judge afterward that there had not been sufficient cause for their irrational outburst. Or regarding the basic anxiousness from which the anger came, an emotionally ill person would typically, within counseling, admit he did not have a clue where that basic anxiety was coming from.

So fellow ministers can see a single behavior that can be described as emotional illness, but does not truly reflect who this person is. Or, see it is not behavior that requires action, such as firing a capable minister. And they justly ignore the one harmless instance.

• INSUFFICIENT REACTIONS BY OBSERVERS OF THE EMOTIONALLY ILL

When fellow ministers or diocesan personnel observe or hear about the ongoing seriously anxious, depressed or irrational behaviors of the emotionally ill minister, their response is often insufficient. When the behavior is serious in its impact or the behaviors of the emotionally ill person persist, some observers "let it slide."

Examples of "letting it slide" include a simple, "Oh, there she goes again, another of her sad days." Or, "I sure wish he would stop drinking, but better that than a sex addiction." Or, from a bishop, "It's a question of numbers; we need enough pastors to fill the slots." Also, many types of emotional illness appear as, or are, addictions. Yet as codependents, we look the other way, we tolerate, we meet our own needs, we excuse them because of their other good qualities, we ignore the evil their behaviors do to others and to ministry.

Another reason for not speaking up is similar to what happens in domestic violence. "Too much is at stake for me if I speak up or otherwise try to do something about the harm being done." Though physical violence is rare in ministry conflict, emotional violence can certainly be present. Alcoholism and other addictions can produce acts of negative emotional tirades, sexual advances and irrational character attacks. All of these threats to self-esteem and peace and general well-being can be ignored if we fear the loss of our job, the loss of our ability to financially survive. Our job can also be an important part of our self-esteem that we fear losing. Or we may actually like the person who is attacking us. For example, we say, "This is a priest who represents God."

• HOW THE EMOTIONALLY ILL GET PAST EVALUATIONS

Now we go to another critical question: How do the emotionally ill get past the evaluations, whether at the seminary, in getting hired and kept on at the parish or diocese, or in volunteer interviews? One answer is in the codependency we have just seen. Other answers are in the myriad of human weaknesses, such as ignorance about emotional illness, procrastination in dealing with real problems and lack of courage and justice in carrying out what needs to be done.

One example is the case of the bishop who ignores the seminary's negative psychological evaluation of a new priest, due to "the need for numbers to fill the positions." Given that a particular evaluation could not pinpoint pedophilia specifically, the emotional illness predicted by the exam should give the bishop pause. After ordination, the man might commit numerous crimes of pedophilia in more than one parish.

In another story, a pastor known by the diocese to be diagnosed as paranoid-schizophrenic might continue such behaviors to the serious emotional harm of a staff member. The diocese provides neither protection nor reinstatement to the staff member.

In both cases, one can believe that ignorance, a lack of justice and a lack of courage have all played a part in the reaction behavior of the storied dioceses. One might further consider such serious lack of courage as a condition or sign of corporate emotional illness.

At the parish level, the autonomy given to pastors by some dioceses can extend to all their hiring and firing behavior. Virtually whole staffs can be let go when an emotionally immature new pastor chooses to bring in his own staff, in spite of the injustice to those very capable ministers already in the parish who possess both a desire to serve the church and a need to financially maintain their families. Also, parishioners can be ignored for years when they have presented to the diocese factual examples of major extortion of their parish funds by a priest who has a gambling addiction, another emotional illness.

Though often not a part of parish procedures, skilled interviews of new volunteers can reveal emotionally ill persons. One looks for the overly anxious, very sad, irrational personality when questioning a prospective volunteer or minister. The potential for harm to ministry by the emotionally ill includes the harm that can come from our volunteer ministers.

In conclusion, we have seen the dark side of ministry in this chapter on emotional illness. The negative impact on the fruitfulness of the emotionally ill themselves, on their victims and on ministries is potentially massive. If the large figure of emotionally ill pastors seriously impacting ministries is accurate (see the Introduction), one could easily question the silence within the United States church about such a reality. Lawsuits brought pedophilia to the table to force action in dealing with that reality. Will civil lawsuits be necessary in this reality of emotional illness? One can envision even class action demands. Financial redress for emotional violence and unjust loss of employment present just two of the future possible examples. Once a case is made, the potential number of victims coming forward could be enormous.

Another concern regarding emotional illness is the impact on the sustainability of lay ministers. Truly, lay ministers are a long-term solution to the declining number of priests. However, will good lay ministers stay in church ministry if the climate of emotional illness—anxiety, depression and irrationality—continues to grow at all levels of administration and ministry?

As we now go on to consider sin as a cause of ministry conflict, we leave behind the other two causes, natural personality differences and emotional illness. But these causes often produce behaviors that are sinful in their impact. Both the victims and the ministries suffer or are destroyed. But so much of the behaviors from the first two causes are separate from conscious, freely chosen sin. So we proceed to examine real sin itself as a cause of ministry conflict.

QUESTIONS FOR DISCUSSION

1. What experiences have I had with people who I thought had been overly anxious, depressed or irrational in their behavior?
2. How did one or more of these instances affect me?
3. In what other ways did their behavior affect my ministry work?

SIN

In the early morning chill, as I walked along our mountain community road with its ponderosas and turquoise sky, I noticed two brown-and-white squirrels in a flower planter next to the road. When I realized they were expensive ceramic squirrels, I wondered at the foolishness of the residents leaving them so exposed. But my next thought was a temptation to take them, thinking of how I could just drive by at night and pick them up. In the end, I chose not to take them. And it is precisely this gap—the division between the temptation and the choosing—that defines sin. Also there are the issues of the seriousness of the crime, our awareness of that seriousness and our freedom-inhibiting emotions in choosing the sin.

But in this chapter, we focus on the harm that intentional sin does to ministry. We have already discussed the evil that sinful behaviors bring upon ministry through the first two causes of natural personality differences and emotional illness. For example, the uncontrolled anger behaviors of the first cause and the irrational anger of the second cause both do serious damage to ministers and ministry. Now, we proceed to a more detailed focus on sin itself, naming the many behaviors of intentional sin. The specific sins we list, when committed, may at times have their roots in the other two causes, but there is a tremendous need in our ministerial culture to simply "name the behavior for the sin it is."

• LISTS OF SINS FROM SAINTS PAUL AND THOMAS AQUINAS

As background to our investigation into the intentional sins that most harm ministry, we turn first to Saint Paul's Letter to the Galatians. He had converted these Gentiles to Christianity only to discover later that Jewish Christians were trying to bring them back to the pharisaical emphasis on the minute anti-sin laws and self-merit that Jesus had opposed. So Paul reminded the Galatians that he had preached the freedom Jesus had brought. Nevertheless, Paul goes on to describe how even in their new freedom of the Spirit they must remember to avoid the "sins of the flesh." As we will see in Paul's list, there are more sins than what we would consider sins of the flesh. Rather, there are at least eight other sins, from "enmities" to "envy," that we know directly concern ministry. "Now the works of the flesh are obvious: fornication, impurity, licentiousness, idolatry, sorcery, enmities, strife, jealousy, anger, quarrels, dissensions, factions, envy, drunkenness, carousing, and things like these" (Galatians 5:19–21).

Then in Saint Thomas Aquinas, we have many additional sins and vices to choose from in measuring sin's harmful impact on ministry. They are listed in Volumes III and IV of his *Summa Theologica*. Here we list, in the order they appear in the *Summa*, those that harm ministry: hatred, sloth, envy, discord, contention, scandal, imprudence, negligence, injustice, reviling, backbiting, tale-bearing, derision, disobedience, ingratitude, vengeance, lying, boasting, flattery, quarreling, covetousness, prodigality, fear, ambition, vainglory, pusillanimity [lack of courage], meanness, vices opposed to perseverance, gluttony, drunkenness, lust, incontinence, anger, cruelty and pride. With these two lists, provided by Paul and Thomas Aquinas, we now prioritize the most important vices in the order of their harmfulness to ministry.

• PRIORITIZING THE SINS THAT CAUSE THE MOST HARM TO MINISTRY

In seeking criteria by which to prioritize the sins that cause the most harm to ministry, two seem the most helpful:

• the sin must be able to do serious harm to ministry,
• the number of ministers or ministries harmed affects the sin's placement on the priority list.

With those criteria in mind, we have listed the following ten sins or categories of sins. They are prioritized from most harmful to least harmful, though all are considered serious threats in their capacity to harm ministry. The first seven are the most harmful in terms of the numbers affected, insofar as they may occur at the diocesan and pastor levels of functioning. The final three are harmful to fewer people as they may occur at the parish level among individual staff and volunteer ministers. Without question, all ten sins can occur at any level of the overall ministry of a diocese.

Pride—The Primary Gateway to Harming Ministry

If one tries to make sense of the news headlines reporting the alleged sins of priests or bishops, pride seems to present itself as a root cause. For example, if it is their own sexual scandal, one may ask what they were thinking. Where was their spirituality? What makes sense is that they were blinded by pride, thinking that in their excellence they were greater than the God who made the rules. "I, as a representative of God, am special. I am so special I can do whatever I want." This inordinate belief in one's own excellence opens wide the door to many other sins, since one has taken on a general contempt for divine law, as Saint Thomas describes pride (*Summa Theologica*, Volume IV, Question 162, Article 2).

Another sin that is related to pride, according to Aquinas's list, is ambition. Ambition creates a tolerance to the administrative sins of those both above and below one's level of ministry. If I as a priest want to become a bishop, my temptation of ambition can cause me to ignore the unjust behaviors of the current bishop who could influence my upward movement. If the current bishop is closing poor parishes in order to have more priests to open new, rich parishes, I may not voice my concern. Or again, if the bishop ignores emotionally ill pastors who fire high-quality staff members, my ambition may well keep me quiet. Connected to this ambition is the desire for power. The more power one has, the greater one's sense of one's own excellence will be.

What are the harmful effects of pride in ministry? We have already seen some examples above. But of primary concern are the numbers affected if pride is present at the higher levels of ministry, such as in the diocesan offices or at the pastor level. Diocesan decisions regarding ministry might affect eighty parishes or upwards of a quarter-million parishioners. A pastor's decisions and behavior might affect 3,000 parishioners. So any behaviors coming from pride and all the resulting other sins, such as ambition and injustice, affect so many more people than just those within an individual ministry. A bishop overly concerned for his own image as a disciplinarian may too quickly withdraw pastors from ministry without getting enough details to make a prudent final judgment as to their behavior. Or a pastor overly concerned for his image as an ultra-conservative may unjustly fire a skilled staff member for what may have been a one-time, inadvertent comment about a particular devotional practice among some of the parishioners.

Injustice—Firing and Poor Hiring Practices

Justice is giving to others what is their right. The sin of injustice that harms ministry has many examples in day-to-day ministry. When it happens at the diocesan or pastoral level, many people and ministries are affected.

If a bishop fires a competent diocesan religious education director rather than dialogue with that director on his or her current difference of vision, then all those ministries are seriously harmed. Broken are the diocesan director's years of established trust and motivation with the parish directors. The ability of that diocescan director to hold each of the parish directors to the full training of their catechists is lost. The spreading ripples of injustice toward children are magnified throughout the diocese by the act of too hastily firing a competent director.

The potential for sins of injustice toward ministry and those ministered to go on and on, whether in the form of sexism, racism, uncontrolled emotional illness or natural personality differences that evolves into fierce fights. For example, a pastor may hire a man to replace a departing parish liturgy director even though a woman who also applied for the job is more competent. Injustice to the woman not only takes place, but the parishioners receive less service than they had a right to. Age, too, can be a justice issue when a diocese, like the worst of corporations, fires a capable staff member who is one year away from full-retirement income.

Or a predominantly Hispanic parish may be closed to free up a priest to open a new parish in a rich, mostly Anglo-Saxon suburb. Those who lost their parish must then travel a much greater distance to find a Spanish Mass.

Scandal—Lust, Greed and Other Addictions

Scandal is a person's word or deed that causes the "spiritual downfall" of another. In terms of numbers affected, scandalous actions at the diocesan or parochial level potentially cause the greatest number of "spiritual downfalls" among the faithful and lay ministers. For example the sins of lust and greed, which may result in pedophilia and embezzlement respectively, scandalize and create headlines. Both sins cause many parishioners to question their spiritual leaders, not to mention the entire church. The serious sin of religious leaders, once it is known, makes no sense to their followers, since it puts in doubt the veracity and the reliability of all that the church says about how one should live. Jesus challenged this very hypocrisy in Matthew 23. It drew his greatest anger, and he tried to offset the scandal right up front by telling the people to follow what their religious teachers teach but not do as they do (v. 3).

Besides creating scandal that drives people away from their faith, lust also impacts ministry in various ways. For example, female or male "groupies" attracted to priests or other ministry leaders may seek romantic or sexual favors. Reasons can include personal sexual satisfaction or the personal power experienced in being closely connected to those perceived to have power. Even financial gain can motivate if the end result is a staff position or increased duties and therefore increased pay. Besides the "groupies," priests and other ministry leaders themselves can initiate all of the above, as can happen in the business world. Parish ministries, where most sins do not stay hidden forever, are affected by both the injustice and the scandal.

Greed scandalizes and therefore affects an individual's faith more than some may realize. The humble and spiritually sophisticated Catholic knows that Jesus' preoccupation was with the least of our brethren. So when a huge $75,000 statue of a priest in his flowing Mass vestments is hung on the outer face of the church, these conscientious Catholics become concerned. They experience scandal at both the possible ego of the pastor and the misuse of funds that could have supported additional ministry to the marginalized of the parish community.

Then there is the expensive car and rich neighborhood of the bishop. Catholics know their own desires for both, and they know these desires represent their unhealthy need to be valued for what they have, not for who they are. They may say, "Since I am important, I have a right to these external proofs of my special value." I remember the saintly, humble pastor of a Lubbock parish whose only transportation was an ancient, very rusty pink Cadillac with its fancy tail fins. He enjoyed driving it around his economically mixed parish that included many wealthy Texas ranchers.

Other sources of scandal are addictions such as alcoholism, drug abuse and gambling. Alcoholism creates behaviors that lead to a lack of control and directly harm parish ministers, such as an alcoholic pastor who often experiences fits of rage and takes it out on his fellow ministers. The ministers, like codependent spouses, end up feeling guilty at the cover-ups they often take part in, and experience the insecurity of not knowing what irrational rage might come next. Gambling addiction can produce embezzlement on the part of a pastor or staff member. For example, a new pastor in his first observable ministry activity posts twenty-five snapshots of elderly women parishioners in his office. The pastor turns out to be dunning them under the auspices of charity for the church, only to keep the money himself. A staff member who observes this may never mention the behavior to the diocese, because of fear or codependence. But years later, after many parishioner complaints, the gambling priest might be pulled from pastorship due to revelation of his alleged forms of embezzlement. But, by that time, the most egregious damage is done to several people on various levels—parishioners, ministers and diocesan leaders.

Lack of Courage—Lack of Ministry Protection

At the diocesan and pastor level, the hiring or keeping on of incompetent directors of diocesan or parish ministries can represent a lack of courage that seriously harms ministry. For example, the diocesan adult faith formation director may have organized an ineffectual system of training and evaluation sessions for his parish-level catechists of adults. For years, few catechists across the diocese attended these sessions. The bishop has challenged this critical incompetence and the injustice done to adult parishioners, but in the end does not fire the incompetent director and the director continues in ministry.

Not having the courage to deal with emotionally ill ministers, as in the widely reported cases of pedophilia, has presented itself as a major problem in the American Catholic church.

Sloth—Procrastination and Negligence

If sloth is a "sluggishness of the mind which neglects to begin good" (*Summa Theologica*, Volume III, Question 35, Article 1, p. 1339), there exists so many examples in ministry at all levels. In Question 54, Article 1, Aquinas adds a similar sin to sloth, negligence, which "denotes lack of due solicitude." This "neglecting to begin good" and "lack of due solicitude" can be seen at both the diocesan and parish levels in the critical lack of adequate ministry training.

For example, diocesan-wide training programs for religious education catechists that draw very few participants mean the children's ministries are seriously harmed by this sloth at the director's level. Rethinking of tools such as better marketing, better monitoring and having more serious consequences for catechists may require capable attention. In other words, aggressive attention, rather than sloth and negligence, may be needed for the essentials of mercy, justice and faith called for by Jesus in his attack on the Pharisees in Matthew 23. But shortly after that attack, Jesus (in the parable of the talents), described how the Master sent the unproductive servant to the place where there is weeping and gnashing of teeth. The servant sinned by allowing fear and sloth to bury his talent.

We see diocese after diocese carry out a visioning process in which they involve many people at all levels. Their desire is good, but the end product can be nothing more than general categories of ministries they want to concentrate on, such as adult faith formation. Yet, annual renewal of prioritized vision, practical objectives and timelines provides a major tool to cut through the sloth, negligence and procrastination that seriously prevent ministry fruitfulness. Also at issue is whether one spends too much time on useless tasks, rather than necessary, productive and meaningful ones.

At a personal level among ministers, a relatively new danger exists in the TV and computer addictions that destroy many hours of the day or week. In the latest abnormal psychology textbooks, Internet addiction is described at length as a specific new pathology. Sloth, negligence and procrastination now have these additional sins in their arsenal for harming ministry.

Factions—Source of Destructive Power

A full eight of the fifteen "sins of the flesh" listed by Paul in Galatians 5:19–21 refer to what can happen between factions at both the diocesan and parish levels of ministry leadership: "enmities, strife, jealousy, anger, quarrels, dissentions, factions, envy..." For now we summarize all that in the one word: *factions*. This grouping of ministers may grow out of power, pride, ambition, territorialism, fear and other human weaknesses.

At the diocesan level, those who want power may try to associate themselves with the bishop, or around one or more naturally powerful personalities in the administration. A true faction can be most noticed in their tendency to listen only to their own counsel. One of the greatest evils of a faction is that the Holy Spirit speaking through other voices of vision or concern in the diocese can be silenced. A bishop without natural decision-making skills of his own may well succumb to the inherently bad counsel of a prideful, self-centered faction.

All of this can impact a pastor and his ministry decision making. One parish group can try to establish a sorely needed new Hispanic ministry. But a faction of racist parishioners, who may be the largest financial contributors, can kill such a program. Or the bishop may decide that three parishes in a relatively small town need to combine into one parish to ease the priest shortage. Suddenly, there may erupt two or three factions based in the different churches who oppose the combination for racist, financial or power-related reasons. The result is that a string of pastors will either ask to leave their post, or worse, they don't ask to leave, and consequently endure grave emotional or physical illnesses because of the incessant insults brought on by the factions' hurtful comments and actions.

Factions can arise even within parish staffs. A typical cause is the arrival of a "new kid on the block" in the form of a new pastor or a new staff person. For example, an old staff person may fear the power of the better-skilled new person, especially if the skills are similar to his or her own. In this case, the invasion of their "turf" can become the issue. Sometimes simple jealousy rears its ugly head. The invaded staff person begins to gather a faction to offset the newcomer's power, rather than welcoming that person's benefit to the overall parish ministry. Later, we will look more closely at such a process in the series of "local parish ministry sins" when we discuss jealousy, hatred, slander, lies, enmity and strife.

Unjust Accusations—Acting on False Information

This brings us to the last of the seven sins for which we have the most concern when they occur at the diocesan or parochial level. At these levels of administration, this sin affects the most ministries and the most people, because it often results in the firing or removal of competent ministers. The primary problem regarding damage to ministry is acting on false information, which is the product of unjust accusations or gossip. The primary way to avoid acting on false information, of course, is to be thorough in getting both sides of the story.

Unjust accusations and false information can come from parishioners or other ministers. The bishop may be told of a pastor who supposedly concelebrated a wedding Mass with an Episcopalian priest, along with rumors of his having mishandled parish finances. So the bishop pulls the priest from his pastorship. Then other parishioners come forward with the actual facts, the other side of the story that could have been gathered with not much more effort, to prove their pastor's innocence. Due to the ease of lying and the power of such sins as jealousy and struggle for power, bishops, diocesan personnel and pastors have a primary responsibility to beware of false information. The "other side of the story" must, in justice, always be diligently searched out before making personnel decisions.

The act of firing based on false information reigns as a great destroyer of ministry. One untruth can also destroy the effectiveness of a minister, and therefore requires extreme vigilance at all levels of church administration.

Envy and Hatred—Source of Other Harmful Sins

Having discussed the seven sins most harmful to ministry both at the diocesan and parish levels of behavior, we come to the three sins most harmful at the local ministry level. A progression exists among these three sins or groups of sins, from jealousy and hatred as the initial sins, to the follow-through behavior of slander and lies to the extreme of total enmity and strife.

Saint Paul had his own problems from the jealousy of others. In Antioch, almost the whole city turned out to "...hear the word of the Lord. But when the Jews saw the crowds, they were filled with jealousy; and blaspheming, they contradicted what was spoken by Paul" (Acts 13:44–45).

Jealousy can arise simply from a "turf" or a territorial problem. One's value may come from one's position as the religious education director of grades one through six. Then the pastor chooses to hire a charismatic new Youth Ministry director, taking away the sixth grade for a new junior high sixth-through-eighth-grade program. The stealing of one's turf, combined with the new person's impressive skills in dealing with youth, can bring on the temptation to become jealous. Giving into the temptation can quickly evolve into hatred of the new minister because one's self-esteem is bruised when his place in the parish community is threatened.

Another example: For years a volunteer RCIA director may have run a great program, but a new pastor brings in his favorite volunteer RCIA director from his former parish. The pastor does nothing to deal with the potential conflict. He lets the two deal with the transition themselves. As a result, hatred grows and the number of those attending the program each year dwindles to half because the parishioners witness the animosity and are reluctant to recommend the RCIA program to relatives and friends.

Slander and Lies—Behavior That Destroys

From jealousy and hatred, we arrive at the behaviors that allow one to follow up on those two sins. Lying and slander make it possible to carry out one's jealousy and hatred. They are also connected, in that both sins come from unhealthy self-esteem being threatened. Lying about another person is the broader of the two sins and covers many different applications. For example, one can lie to the pastor that another, disliked minister said bad things about the pastor. Or one can lie that the disliked minister does not carry her fair share of the ministry burden.

Slander can involve lying, but is specifically the malicious and defamatory statement about a person that is designed to injure his or her good name. By making defamatory attacks on the reputation of the disliked person, one can try through slander to reduce the power of the minister or to feel that one is better than the one slandered. Unchallenged slander can seriously harm the ability of the minister to function as a leader and thereby harms the ministry that person leads. People are less likely to follow the leadership or to use the services of those attacked.

The slandered minister can be powerfully affected, becoming less energetic and effective as a leader. Motivation suffers. The minister can experience a lack of self-value as well as powerlessness, which was the intention of the slanderer. This effort to harm the reputation of a minister can come from the diocesan level, where a diocesan leader has experienced a confrontation with a parish leader who challenges one of the practices of his diocesan ministry. The diocesan leader may give into the temptation to share with other diocesan heads derogatory information to slander the skills of the parish leader.

As in the case of unjust accusations discussed earlier, there can be an unfortunate lack of courage on the part of ministers to speak up with the truth when a fellow minister is slandered or lied about. Speaking up in the face of defamation of a person's good name remains one of the most necessary and typical ministry obligations.

Enmity and Strife—The Infighting

Enmity and strife represent the ongoing battle, the constant infighting that can so greatly vitiate the good works of a parish. As stated, one of the major causes of strife is the jealousy and hatred that finds expression in the behavior of lies and slander. All the other sins we dealt with can also enter in as causes and perpetuation of the infighting. Besides the sins, there also exist the two other major causes of conflict: natural personality differences and emotional illness. Here we are concerned with the infighting at the parish level, but such conflict goes all the way to the top, with, for example, the Vatican personnel in conflict with theologians and other ministers internationally.

All the way through our discussion of sin in this chapter, we have seen many instances of the enmity and strife that sin produces, and all contribute to conflict in parish ministry. But in the enmity and strife in the parish, a major element is remaining stuck in the conflict. Often, parish ministers caught up in conflict do not choose to end the battle. The damage goes on, with capable ministers leaving or being fired, with ministries bearing little fruit. The life of the parish withers to a dried-out shell due to the enmity and strife.

The most frustrating thing about all the ten areas of sin is the lack of courage, at every level, whether diocesan, clerical or individual parish ministry. If a lack of courage was replaced by courage, all these sins we have discussed would be dealt with, and ministries at every level could flourish. We have dealt with all three causes of conflict in ministry: natural personality differences, emotional illness and sin. Now we have the joy of moving on to the magnificent solutions of Jesus. Each of his solutions resolves all three of these causes of conflict.

QUESTIONS FOR DISCUSSION

1. Which of these sins have I seen harm either my ministry or the ministry of others?

2. What sins other than those prioritized in this chapter have I seen harm ministry?

3. Who do I hold responsible for doing something about each of these kinds of sins?

LOVING SERVANTHOOD

As I look out on the national forest from my desk, I see a panorama of God's loving servanthood toward all of the world's children, including those of us in religious ministry. The huge green ponderosas, the blue sky with the floating clouds, the yellow and purple spring flowers are all designed for us to enjoy. These trees produce our homes, other trees give us fruit. Redheaded woodpeckers drive off the squirrel trying to steal their sunflower seeds from my bird feeder trough near the woodpeckers' tree. God serves our needs and we serve the needs of others. Out of love for us, God models the servanthood we should in turn practice. We are now leaving the chapters of ministry conflict examples behind us to go on to the joy of considering such solutions to conflict as this servanthood that Jesus teaches us.

• LOVING SERVANTHOOD IN SCRIPTURE

Servanthood as the first of Jesus' solutions to ministry conflict finds expression in this one simple statement: "The greatest among you will be your servant" (Matthew 23:11). Jesus makes this recommendation to the Pharisees, during the week before they see to his death. Knowing their intent, he nevertheless starts this final effort to solve the conflict between himself and them. He tries to get the top religious leaders to understand that God's way of exercising authority is the same way that God functions toward us—in total love—by showing us how meeting our needs as a servant meets the needs of the master. In Matthew 22, just shortly before the scene in the temple, the Pharisees had asked

Jesus, "Teacher, which commandment in the law is the greatest?" (v. 36). Jesus replied with the greatest two commandments: loving God and your neighbor as yourself (vv. 37–40). Now, with his short "The greatest among you will be your servant," Jesus spells out to them how religious leaders need to practice these commandments of love.

Even earlier, Jesus, in response to the mother of the sons of Zebedee, who wanted high seats of authority for her sons, told his disciples, "...and whoever wishes to be first among you must be your slave; just as the Son of Man came not to be served but to serve, and to give his life a ransom for many" (Matthew 20:27–28).

Mark also states this theme of servanthood in his Gospel: "Whoever wants to be first must be last of all and servant of all" (Mark 9:35). Paul gives us some more details, saying "And the Lord's servant must not be quarrelsome but kindly to everyone, an apt teacher, patient, correcting opponents with gentleness" (2 Timothy 2:24). Opponents, those with whom we fellow-ministers are in conflict, must receive loving gentleness as an exercise of our servanthood. Paul sums up this call from Jesus to religious leaders by saying "yet I have made myself a slave to all" (1 Corinthians 9:19).

Then again later on in this week, on the day we now call Holy Thursday, Jesus would share with his apostles at the Last Supper a striking image of servanthood (John 13:3–20). With the washing of their feet, which Peter strongly objected to at first, Jesus left an indelible image of what humble, loving servanthood means. To explain why he had done this, Jesus said,

> Do you know what I have done to you? You call me Teacher and Lord—and you are right, for that is what I am. So if I, your Lord and Teacher, have washed your feet, you also ought to wash one another's feet. For I have set you an example, that you also should do as I have done to you (John 13:12–15).

Catholics in parishes across the United States profoundly experience the sacramental beauty of both humbly washing the feet of others and having their own washed during Mass on Holy Thursday. There is something very special about this symbolic rite of lovingly serving the needs of others and being served oneself. It is here at the Last Supper that we see Jesus' core teaching of love and servitude in action.

• SERVANTHOOD AS THE PRACTICAL APPLICATION OF LOVING YOUR NEIGHBOR

Servants must meet the needs of their master. Jesus uses this imagery in so many of his parables, as in the parable of the talents, when the master leaves the servants to do something worthwhile with the money that he leaves with them. At the very core of Jesus' teaching is: *Love God and your neighbor as yourself.* What *is* love? Love is wishing good to another. To love is to meet the needs of another. The most practical expression of loving another is servanthood. It is saying, "As a servant I will meet your needs." And, when you experiment with this concept of servanthood, it is simple to find daily ways to practice this attitude and behavior. "Love your neighbor" is abstract. "Respond to the needs of your neighbor like a servant would" gets very specific. Suddenly, loving your neighbor becomes very concrete. You have to look for his or her needs, and you have to lovingly respond to them. You are called by God to wash another's feet—in other words, to serve. And no one is exempt—even the leader is called to be a loving servant.

A priest friend of mine for years has given me his full attention whenever we meet. He maintains contact by e-mail. He is always available when I take the initiative to meet with him. I call it a generosity of spirit, a sign of grace. Jesus would call it servanthood. Pope John Paul II was noted for how open and present he was to whomever he was dealing with at the moment.

As another example of servanthood in our ministry, you may come into a parish as a new youth minister and experience an immediate conflict with an apparently jealous staff minister. You discover that minister is deriding your new registration package that was created for sign-ups in September. You know the package is efficient and sufficient. So you choose to investigate. This disgruntled minister had the junior high students as part of her ministry before you came along, and you were given both the junior and senior high youth. This unhappy minister also has much less natural charisma in dealing with youth, which may also cause the jealousy. In looking at the needs of this other minister, you notice that, with her new RCIA responsibility, she is desperately looking for more speakers. Servanthood suggests that you volunteer to help as one of the speakers until she gets fully underway.

Another example of the "quick to help out" servanthood personality is the children's religious education director who can always be counted on to help in small and immediate projects. Yet she knows exactly where to draw the line in order to meet her own ministry's responsibilities. When she cannot help, she turns to her own volunteers, who are also taught a servanthood spirituality, to find someone to help the other ministry.

Servanthood also reflects the need God has for instruments of the Father's loving care of everyone. God cannot personally teach the little ones about God. We must do the learning, experiencing and teaching about God, while becoming God's face, voice and wisdom. It is an extraordinary calling—this modeling of who God is—by humbly serving as God's instrument of love.

• GOD'S SERVANTHOOD TOWARD US

To support our humble acceptance of servanthood as a principle of ministry leadership and as a solution to ministry conflict, we need to recognize God's servanthood toward us. How can we not do as our Lord has said, "as I have done to you" (John 13:15)? The huge oak tree gives us shade. The apricot tree gives us luscious fruit. The red rose gives us beauty in sight, touch and smell. God gives us the friendship and love of other persons. God's graces give us light and strength and promise of a glorious eternity in an everlasting love relationship. God loves each and every one of us each day in a constant servanthood of meeting our needs. Jesus put it all in the simple words of the Our Father, "Give us this day our daily bread" (Matthew 6:11).

Why does God do this? God loves us. The God of the physical universe administers to our needs constantly. The first principle of reality is loving God, each other and ourselves. We practice this as servants ministering to the Master's needs, other's needs and our own. How can we do less? This is the simple nature of love shown to us by God.

Another reality of God's loving servanthood includes Jesus' insistence that the Father will take care of us: "[H]ow much more will your Father in heaven give good things to those who ask him!" (Matthew 7:11). Jesus also extends his own loving servanthood to his apostles and to us, stating that after going to the Father, "I will do whatever you ask in my name, so that the Father may be glorified in the Son. If in my name you ask me for anything, I will do it" (John 14:13–14).

• THANKFULNESS AND HUMILITY—COROLLARIES TO SERVANTHOOD
God's servanthood toward us obviously clamors for our gratefulness. Is this thankfulness we experience also a reflection of how God is? No doubt thankfulness happens between the Father, the Son and the Holy Spirit. Made in the image and likeness of God, the thankfulness of our human spirit most likely reflects their relationship. When a person seeks your goodness and loves you, your response is thankfulness. A corollary to this must be God's thankfulness toward us for the good we do to others for God's sake and theirs. Servanthood includes this huge round of thankfulness among God, others and ourselves. In practice, this requires our daily expression of thanks to God and others and our gracious acceptance of their thanks to us.

Humility also connects to servanthood in this strong statement of Paul: "Do nothing from selfish ambition or conceit, but in humility regard others as better than yourselves. Let each of you look not to your own interests, but to the interests of others" (Philippians 2:3–4).

As we have noted, looking to the interests of others is the definition of servanthood. Paul speaks to leaders, noting their natural temptation to "selfish ambition or conceit," but rightly encourages an attitude of humility and servanthood.

Jesus had his own words of God's wisdom for the disciples regarding humility. "Truly I tell you, unless you change and become like children, you will never enter the kingdom of heaven. Whoever becomes humble like this child is the greatest in the kingdom of heaven" (Matthew 18:3–4). We thus have one more description of the least becoming the greatest in Jesus' mandate to his religious ministers-to-be. Jesus again connects humility to servanthood as he reacts to his apostles arguing among themselves who was the greatest. "He sat down, called the twelve, and said to them, 'Whoever wants to be first must be last of all and servant of all.' Then he took a little child and put it among them" (Mark 9:35–36).

What we have been seeing here is that both Jesus and Paul recognize the psychological difficulty for leaders who, by their God-given talent, want to be in charge, to be the one listened to, to be the one most valued in relationship to others. Pride of position is a natural temptation for leaders. Jesus and Paul, therefore, strongly emphasize to ministry leaders the need for humility. Leaders accept their leadership position in the world as those who must model God and who, out of love, serve. Being attentive to the needs of others before our own needs, like a servant, correctly models God's love and humbly reflects the truth of who God is.

Another possibility regarding humility as a minister may be the need for fear in our responsibility to God. If humility is acknowledging the truth about who we are, then a healthy fear should exist regarding our responsibility to be servants to others. God expects us to serve the needs of others first and foremost. For example, we do not achieve that end by an authoritarian "I will tell you all you need to know" mindset as leaders. Instead, finding out others' needs through a humane, logical dialogue is a major principle of practicing our responsibility. Authoritarian-tempted leaders need to live in the fear of meeting their God who eventually will say, "I was a stranger and you did not welcome me" (Matthew 25:43).

Another need for humility among authoritarian-tempted leaders concerns the concept of truth. To say that I have all the truth and you cannot add anything to that through dialogue is to succumb to a "pride of position" temptation to sin. That pride forgets that all worthwhile truth is profound and grows in its understanding. That understanding has blossomed through centuries of dialogue among all the members of the Body through whom the Holy Spirit resides and speaks.

• Servanthood as a Preference for the Poor

The life of Jesus as a religious minister reflects his concern for those most in need. The lepers, the tax collectors, the prostitutes, the blind, those of different faiths—like the Samaritan woman at the well and the Roman centurion's daughter—were all outcasts. The Jewish culture of the time did not accept them, did not want to listen to or service their need for even human acceptance. The exception was Jesus, God. This predilection for the "poor," the unloved and the despised, remains a problem of ministry in our own day. Yet each of us as ministers must model God's love and speak up for a very active servanthood toward all who have the most need among our relatives, our parish and our community.

Concrete examples abound of what we can do to maintain this emphasis in our servanthood. We need to choose, if we have not done so already, some way to serve each day. The habit must become permanent. For example, we can volunteer for the Saint Vincent de Paul Society or in a food-service line for the homeless. A friend of mine who is a religious education director buys extra groceries each week when she shops for herself so she can bring some bags to the parish food bank. A psychologist friend always has nonperishable food in the back seat of his car to give to the war veteran or homeless person waiting at

the freeway off-ramp. Some love to take the time to approach an out-
cast for a few moments of friendly but safe conversation. Others keep
half of their tithing to spend on whatever need comes up. They love the
monthly ability to spontaneously help out "where the Spirit blows."

• SERVANTHOOD AS A SOLUTION TO EACH OF THE THREE CAUSES OF
CONFLICT
In chapter two, when I first discussed servanthood as a solution to conflict ministry, I described in detail how servanthood helps resolve each
of the three causes of conflict. Primarily, natural personality differences find resolution in the ministers working to be open and responsive to each other's needs, even when, for example, they both want to
be in charge. Both can listen to the views of the other minister until
they reach an agreement, based on the best of their combined facts or
judgments. Also, servanthood helps in dealing with another minister's
emotional illness. The interest a loving servant leader shows to an
emotionally ill person can greatly reduce anxiety levels. Even ministers
in sin discover a greater good in the love and friendship extended to
them. In fact, this may also be God's love extended to the sinner
through this human instrument of servanthood. Amazingly, each of
the causes of ministry conflict submits to the logic of servanthood.

• PRACTICAL APPLICATIONS FOR SERVANTHOOD IN MINISTRY
CONFLICT SPIRITUALITY
Once we accept the necessity of servanthood in our belief system, we
need practical applications for our ministry conflict spirituality. As you
experiment with applying the concept of servanthood to your daily
ministry life, you will come up with a growing number of logical applications that you already practice or can add. The following are some
suggestions:

  • Remember the primary question of servanthood: "What are the
    needs or concerns of this person or this group?" The second is,
    "What can I do to meet those needs?"

- As a ministry leader committed to servanthood, your toughest task may be to humbly place the needs of others first, as God does, out of love.

- If another leader wants to be a decision maker in a mutual task with you, ask for and carefully listen to their judgment on the situation.

- Recognize the turf or territory of other ministers by supporting their final decision in their area of responsibility.

- Each time you meet someone, look for, ask about and discern what his or her immediate interests may be and respond to those.

- Avoid the trap of doing "all their deeds to be seen by others" which Jesus directly opposes with "the greatest among you will be your servant" (Matthew 23:5, 11).

- With an emotionally ill minister, respond with peaceful friendship to reduce his or her anxiety and meet his or her needs.

- In the face of the sin of slander against you, forgive the minister first in your heart. Show signs of forgiveness in the loving friendliness you extend to him.

- Pray to Jesus for the grace of practicing servanthood toward those you come into conflict with in ministry.

- ## SOME DIFFICULTIES IN SERVANTHOOD

Three difficulties come to mind when we try to practice servanthood: 1) the natural resistance in a leader to submit to others; 2) the fellow-ministers who do not return the favor of servanthood even after it is extended to them; and, 3) the issue of God's commandment to love ourselves.

Regarding the first difficulty—the natural resistance of a leader to submit to others: A leader often has that God-given talent of decision making. This skill includes wanting to be the one in charge, to be aggressive, to listen to one's own judgment and needs. Jesus and Saint Paul recognized the natural instincts of leaders and emphasized the need for humility in leaders, demonstrated by listening to the needs of others and practicing servanthood. Nevertheless, the temptations to over-control, to seek one's own needs first, to fall prey to "pride of position" and ignore the judgments of others in dialogue can lead to sinning against servanthood. Servanthood remains as a primary antidote to the temptations of leaders in ministry, who naturally gravitate to such positions.

The second difficulty of servanthood is a common one. Even though one practices servanthood and attends to the needs of others, it can hurt when our fellow-minister seems oblivious to our reasonable needs in ministry. For example, what happened to the spirit of "share and share alike" when it comes to facility use? What happened to their being open to helping out when I am in a pinch? Why does he slander me to others when I never speak ill of his weaknesses? Servanthood can be unfair, even a cross. That last word needs to remind us of Jesus' cross. Suffering became a major part of his servanthood ministry. "But I say to you, Love your enemies and pray for those who persecute you, so that you may be children of your Father in heaven; for he makes his sun rise on the evil and on the good, and sends rain on the righteous and the unrighteous" (Matthew 5:44–45). We need to continue our rain or soft-falling snow of goodness on the shoulders of our fellow-ministers who do not respond to our servanthood.

The last difficulty I will discuss regards the commandment of loving ourselves. Saint Paul seems to forget this commandment when he says, "Do nothing from selfish ambition or conceit," the temptations of leadership talent, "but in humility regard others as better than yourselves. Let each of you look not to your own interests, but to the interests of others. Let the same mind be in you that was in Christ Jesus...taking the form of a slave...to the point of death—even death on a cross" (Philippians 2:3–8). This quote of Paul reflects his great awareness of the natural leadership temptations and is effective in describing works here that will strongly offset such human, natural weakness. Asked about the contradiction, Paul would certainly also support the reality of God's affirmation to love ourselves. No doubt he would call us to pray continually to the Holy Spirit for the light and strength to make good judgments in our lives and to love our neighbor as ourselves. Even Jesus had difficulty with this reconciliation, such as when he felt he was not ready to perform the miracle of providing a huge amount of wine at the wedding at Cana. But he deferred to Mary's judgment that it was time for him to begin his ministry.

QUESTIONS FOR DISCUSSION

1. What behaviors of Jesus are examples of loving servanthood?
2. With what daily behaviors could I practice loving servanthood?
3. What are some examples of Mary being of service to others throughout her life?

LOGIC

Logic reigns as a commonsense and practical solution to ministry conflict. One minister of religious education, in reflecting back over the years, found three instances where logic had brought her peace in the face of conflict. Each time, her use of logic caused her to shake the dust off her sandals and move on to a new ministry position.

In the first instance, she spent a year gathering facts about the criminal behavior of a staff member, based on her own observations and reports from parishioners. She shared with the pastor all along such behaviors as money theft from the office, theft in ushering at the Sunday collections and lying about personal hardships in order to collect money from elderly parishioners as well as threats and actual physical assaults directed at the pastor, herself and parishioners.

At the end of the year, the minister took the accumulation of facts to a criminal attorney who verified that sufficient evidence existed for criminal charges. But the attorney warned that the pastor would have to be the one to bring the charges and remove this staff person. Presented with the attorney's conclusion, the pastor refused to act, himself having been threatened. The minister thought that she needed to take a stand. She threatened to quit in protest. And when no change occurred by the end of the month, she ultimately did leave her position.

In the second instance of using logic to resolve ministry conflict, this same minister of religious education agreed to take a position in a different parish following a two-day dialogue with her new pastor-to-be.

From early on in the discussion, she was concerned about the pastor's penchant for micromanagement and even possible emotional illness. Again and again, in the face of specific questions on her part, he promised that he would trust her skills in the details of her work and would not micromanage. Nevertheless, the new pastor's micromanagement began almost immediately and continued for months. Finally, this minister resigned, but before leaving, she trained a new director for the position, one who was used to accepting total compliance.

As to the third instance of needing to trust her logical intelligence, this minister in later life retired and resided in a parish where two successive pastors never responded to her offer to be of service. She had multiple degrees and years of experience in ministry, including conducting training seminars for parishes. After a year of patience with these pastors—offering to work for low pay or even to conduct seminars without a fee—she decided that she needed to go elsewhere. In the words of Jesus in training his apostles, "If anyone will not welcome you or listen to your words, shake off the dust from your feet as you leave that house or town" (Matthew 10:14).

In all three instances, this capable minister employed both logic and intuition while dealing with circumstances of conflict. She prayed for light in her thinking and strength to follow through on her decisions. Other ministers might have come to different conclusions. After months, even years, of observing and gathering facts, this minister followed her own heart. Through logic, supported by prayer for light and strength, she made decisions that maintained her integrity. In retrospect, each judgment to leave proved an accurate response, giving her even greater peace as she looked back.

• THE IMPORTANCE OF LOGIC IN SPIRITUALITY

What does logic have to do with spirituality? In the examples above, we saw how the minister needed to use her intelligence in coping with ministry conflict. Her ministry was the instrument of her spirituality. Spirituality, by definition, describes our spirit's way of seeking personal relationship with God and with our fellow human beings. The decisions she made followed a long period of fact gathering and pondering "them in her heart," as Mary did in dealing with her life with her son (Luke 2:19). Intelligent decisions, based on fact and logical judgment, provide us with vision and practical direction for our ministry work. Logic, then, is essential in carrying out our relationship with God and others in ministry.

For a moment, we need to deal with a broader definition of logic. When we say logic is a solution for ministry conflict, we include not only the step-by-step sense of logic, but all the functions of our intellect. Creative intuition and the artistic use of the intellect are included in this broader definition. Thus, we are talking about that power of the human spirit, formed in the image and likeness of God, to discern truth. This power given to us by God needs to be trusted in human life. In *The Ascent of Mount Carmel*, Saint John of the Cross emphasizes the intellect's importance in stating that God "is ever desirous that insofar as possible people take advantage of their own reasoning powers. All matters must be regulated by reason save those of faith" (Kavanaugh and Rodriguez, *The Collected Works of Saint John of the Cross*, p. 235).

In emphasizing that we need to listen to our reasoning powers, John of the Cross challenges those who would listen to some "voice" from God or the Holy Spirit. He says God spoke to us in the Old Testament times, but now expects us to use our own good judgment. Saint Teresa of Avila, another spiritual doctor of the church, joins John of the Cross in insisting on the use of the intellect in our spiritual life, versus listening to "visions and voices" in our decision making. In *The Interior Castle*, she again and again warns her sisters that these are the imagination talking, saying, "resist them [these visions and voices of the imagination] always" (Kavanaugh and Rodriguez, *Collected Works of St. Teresa of Avila*, p. 372).

Yet, we can find a bishop in our own day suggesting in both the Catholic and secular press that the Holy Spirit directly tells him what directions the diocese should take in its planning. This represents not the reasoning and logic of John of the Cross or Teresa of Avila, but rather a dangerous example for both Catholics and others of how to relate to God and others in one's spirituality. If a bishop or priest or other minister thinks he hears the communications of the Holy Spirit, he should at least keep such unusual experiences to himself, or better yet, "resist them always," so as to not teach unsound spirituality that hints of an authoritarian need to control the people. The truth is that, though we pray to the Holy Spirit every day for light, we trust that the Spirit of truth is there within, helping us. There is no waiting around to "hear the voice of God."

• LOGIC'S PLACE IN SCRIPTURE

The Holy Spirit has a powerful role in our ministry spirituality. At the Last Supper, Jesus promised his apostles, "And I will ask the Father, and he will give you another Advocate, to be with you forever. This is the Spirit of truth, whom the world cannot receive, because it neither sees him nor knows him. You know him, because he abides with you, and he will be in you" (John 14: 16–17). And again, "When the Advocate comes, whom I will send to you from the Father, the Spirit of truth who comes from the Father, he will testify on my behalf" (John 15: 26). This Spirit provides us with the truth that our intellect searches out, albeit as a hidden presence. At the center of our decision making, the Spirit is constantly present, wanting us to ask for assistance in searching out the truth. This Spirit is also the God of love that Jesus reminds us to ask for. The same Spirit supports the two functions of the human spirit and spirituality to search out and know with our intellect and to love with our will.

Thus, we see logic's place in ministry spirituality, getting at the truth with the power of the Spirit within us. Logic then has a rightful place in Jesus' solutions to ministry conflict. Also, in the prior chapter on the solution of loving servanthood and in the chapter to come on the solution of loving forgiveness, we learn that we have the same "Advocate Spirit" within us as the source of the loving side of those two additional solutions.

In a final note regarding logic and its truth, Jesus stated, "I am the way, and the truth, and the life" (John 14:6). Jesus, God the Son, has shown us the way by his life of servanthood on earth. He sends us truth—God the Holy Spirit—the source of our truth that we pursue with our intellect, or logic.

Finally, Jesus introduced us to our Father, the source of all life. And the Father is also the source of God's forgiveness, like "the mother hen" of Chapter 23 in Matthew. So Jesus brings us not only the Trinity in himself, but these three persons of God amazingly bring us the corresponding three solutions to ministry conflict provided to us by Jesus in Matthew 23. The *way* is servanthood (the Son), the *truth* is logic (the Holy Spirit) and the *life* is forgiveness (the Father).

• PETITIONING FOR LIGHT AND STRENGTH—THE COROLLARY TO LOGIC
As thankfulness and humility were corollaries or connected practices to servanthood, so asking God for light and strength is a necessary practice in resolving conflict logically. We have seen the source of truth inside us, God the Spirit. As we use our logic to solve conflict solutions, we must ask for the light to understand what to do, and for the strength to follow through on the solutions we figure out. Real spirituality tries to be more and more conscious of that presence, that source of light and strength promised us.

Many ministers go to Mass during the week to draw on that promised source of light and strength. One can offer up one's current ministry conflicts with the presiding priest as he raises Jesus' sacrifice of himself to the Father. Communion becomes a time to place the conflicts in Jesus' hands, asking for the light and strength to solve problems and carry out effective solutions. The strength of the intellect, with God's strength, can provide hope and even immediate peace.

• PRACTICAL APPLICATIONS OF LOGIC IN MINISTRY CONFLICT SPIRITUALITY

Let's consider some specific daily applications of logic as a spiritual solution to ministry conflict. You will experience many applications as you go through your ministry day. Look for ways to practice this logic of Jesus, this looking for the truth in conflict situations, including prayer to the Spirit. Here are some suggestions:

- Always ask questions of yourself and others. This forces the intellect to function, to search for the truth, the facts and the answers. Questioning is a learned skill. Like anything, it takes practice.
- Look for as much detail or as many facts as you can gather. This includes how you and others involved in the conflict are specifically feeling and thinking.
- Based on all the facts you have gathered, ask yourself: What steps make the most logical sense to resolve this conflict?
- After you attempt using step-by-step or fact-based logic, put your creative intuition to work. Think of unique solutions. Give your imagination free rein for the moment.
- Sit on your solution for a day, a week or even a month. Come back and rethink. If the result is the same, you have greater assurance of the solution's validity.
- Be constant in how you ask the Holy Spirit for truth. But remember, you are the one who is responsible for making and trying the conflict solution.

• LOGIC AS A SOLUTION TO EACH OF THE THREE CAUSES OF CONFLICT

The most exciting attribute of Jesus' own use of logic is how it resolves all three causes of ministry conflict. All three causes yield to logic, whether they are natural personality differences, emotional illness or sin. If we are in conflict with another ministry leader over whose judgment will be followed, logic will suggest a number of possible avenues. One way might involve working out a compromise that uses the best of both judgments. With both ministers open to getting at the truth by using logic or creative intuition in dialogue, the chances for reducing conflict are great.

The application of logic to conflicts spurred on by emotional illness cuts through and dissipates irrationality and anxiety. If one minister challenges the other's fears, providing logical proofs that the anxiety is unfounded, or that the depression does not make sense, healing can come. The skill of a trained counselor can best assist the emotionally ill person to search for and find the logical solutions to their illness.

In regards to sin as a source of ministry conflict, logic forces one to ask pivotal questions such as: "What are the natural consequences of this sin?" "What effect is this sin having on another or myself?" Jesus' question to the Pharisees about their sin of wanting to kill him was quite straight, "How can you escape being sentenced to hell?" (Matthew 23:33).

One principle of using logic to resolve sin-created conflict is that all questions trying to break through that sin may produce resistance. Therefore, one must look for a loving, nonjudgmental choice of words for one's logical questions.

Another principle is that the truth may not seem to make an impact now, but logic is like a seed that often grows into effective change.

QUESTIONS FOR DISCUSSION

1. In what situations have you used logic to solve a ministry conflict?
2. In what ministry conflict situation have you used intelligent, creative intuition?
3. Which of your current ministry situations needs further resolution through the application of logic or intuition?

LOVING FORGIVENESS

On a hot summer afternoon, the parish staff gathered for their weekly meeting. The upcoming ministry fair was first on the agenda. Paul was in charge, for the second year, of trying to get more volunteers for parish ministries. Last year produced only a few volunteers for the parish office. So after a brief presentation by Paul as to how the fair would be organized, the pastor, Father John, offered a heartfelt suggestion. "How about we divide up the names of those who sign up and personally call them within a week to come in for an interview?" But the pastor only got through the first half of that suggestion. Paul cut him off with a loud, long sentence directed to Joan, the liturgist, across the table. When Father John tried to finish his suggestion, Paul continued his statement to Joan regarding a prior suggestion of hers. Father John restated it after Paul had finished his dialogue with Joan. When Father John had finished his suggestion about the follow-up phone calls and interviews, Paul quickly discounted the wisdom of either practice, saying the first would take too much time, and composing interviews was something nobody knew how to do.

Paul's disregard and then immediate dismissal of Father John's suggestions was not only rude, but hurtful. But these "hurts" are the everyday stuff of ministry conflict. Whether unintentional or intentional, we nevertheless harm one another in ministry. Jesus, with his always practical wisdom, accurately included in that daily prayer to the Father, "[F]orgive us our debts, as we also have forgiven our debtors" (Matthew 6:12).

Father John, in the ministry conflict described previously, needed to forgive. He recognized he had been harmed. The high-control needs of Paul were out of control. Cutting Father John off was rude. By not listening to the possible wisdom of his suggestions, Paul ignored Father John's value as a contributor to the parish process and withheld the goodness Father John had a right to experience.

To withhold goodness from a person is to do them harm. The opposite of that, of course, is to love, which is to wish good for another. Once the harm has been done, only loving forgiveness will "make the world right again." The word *loving* is key, because that is where forgiveness naturally comes from—loving the person who has harmed us. Father John needs an immediate, interior spiritual response to heal the evil done to him. That response is loving forgiveness, which restores the right order of love to the relationship.

This chapter on loving forgiveness also brings us to God the Father and the connection to ministry conflict. In his first solution to ministry conflict, Jesus as the Son of God introduced us to servanthood. He showed us the way to solve ministry conflict through loving service to others as their "servant." In Jesus' second solution, that of logic, we witnessed God the Holy Spirit as the source of truth that gives light to our intellect to help resolve ministry conflict. Finally, we come to God the Father as the source of the third way to resolve ministry conflict—loving forgiveness. It is God the Father who both lovingly forgives and shares that power with us.

• THE IMPORTANCE OF LOVING FORGIVENESS IN SCRIPTURE
Examples of loving forgiveness in sacred Scripture abound. There is the ever-popular story of the prodigal son that Jesus himself tells, in which the father forgives his errant child (Luke 15:11–32). Then there is the story of Jesus and the Samaritan woman at the well. Jesus asks her to change her ways and leave her life of sin behind to follow him and believe, and she does (John 4:1–42). There is also the story of the woman caught in adultery. Jesus says to the crowd about to stone her,

"Let anyone among you who is without sin be the first to throw a stone at her" (John 8:7). Of course, everyone drops their stones and walks away. Jesus then turns to the woman to forgive her and says, "Neither do I condemn you. Go your way, and from now on do not sin again." (John 8:11). Even at the hour of his own death, Jesus looking down upon his murderers from the crucifix says, "Father, forgive them; for they do not know what they are doing" (Luke 23:34). Jesus not only forgives, he does not condemn, remind or berate in the process of doing so. He forgives selflessly, quickly and lovingly without excuse, patronization or contempt. Jesus himself shows us how loving forgiveness works time and time again. Jesus shows God's loving forgiveness not only for supposedly "chosen" people, but for all people—gentiles, Jews, saints, sinners, Samaritans, and yes, even the Pharisees. His forgiveness knows no bounds. It is unconditional. It is constant and unending. Forgiveness is borne of love. Love is why we forgive. Mercy certainly also represents love, as we see in God speaking to Moses about "a God merciful and gracious, slow to anger, and abounding in steadfast love…for the thousandth generation, forgiving iniquity and transgression and sin" (Exodus 34:6–7).

As God forgives, so must we in ministry. Saint Paul joins all of this together with "just as the Lord has forgiven you, so you also must forgive. Above all, clothe yourselves with love, which binds everything together in perfect harmony" (Colossians 3:13–14). How often must we forgive? When Peter asks if he should forgive a church member as many as seven times, Jesus replies, "Not seven times, but, I tell you, seventy-seven times" (Matthew 18:22).

Even Jesus needed to be forgiven—or at least his actions needed to be understood—by Mary. In Luke, twelve-year-old Jesus leaves his mother and father and causes them great distress. "When his parents saw him they were astonished; and his mother said to him, 'Child, why have you treated us like this? Look, your father and I have been searching for you in great anxiety'" (2:48). For three days Jesus had harmed his parents by causing them "great anxiety" as to his whereabouts. Talk about withholding goodness! Mary needed to forgive Jesus. But, in order to do so, she needed to understand his actions better. She understood, as we also understand in the field of psychology today, that the greatest aid to forgiving someone is to search out the reason they have harmed us. For Mary, it made no sense to her that Jesus would deliberately harm her or her husband. Therefore, she asked, "Why?"

She learns that Jesus was among his peers, the religious leaders of his time, and he was doing his father's work. Thus, he replied, "Why were you searching for me? Did you not know that I must be in my Father's house?" (Luke 2:49) Though Mary and Joseph did not understand what he had just said, at least Mary now knew the reason for his hurtful behavior. Now she could forgive him. Mary points out this all-important step of "Why?" In our own conflicts in ministry, we need not always ask the question directly as she did, but we need to try to answer it for ourselves. Forgiveness becomes much easier as we practice this skill. The effort of intelligent discernment provides greater freedom for us to move on to forgiveness.

Another important element of forgiveness is realizing that before we pray to the Father for anything, we must first forgive. In Mark, Jesus tells us,

> So I tell you, whatever you ask for in prayer, believe that you have received it, and it will be yours. Whenever you stand praying, forgive, if you have anything against anyone; so that your Father in heaven may also forgive you your trespasses. (11:24–25)

The first of these two verses tells us we can get anything we pray to the Father for. But the second verse reminds us that before we pray for anything, we must forgive anyone who has hurt us. This brings us back to the necessity of forgiving people daily for all the harm against us that inevitably occurs in ministry work. Hurts, we have already discussed, are inevitable. So if we intend to pray to God for our own forgiveness, we must first forgive all others.

One of the most essentials gifts of loving forgiveness is the peace it brings to those forgiven as well as to those who forgive. "Peace be with you. As the Father has sent me, so I send you....Receive the Holy Spirit. If you forgive the sins of any, they are forgiven them; if you retain the sins of any, they are retained" (John 20:21–25). We know the experience of peace from the sacrament of penance. In ministry conflict, forgiveness is basic in resolving conflict and bringing about peace. When we pray the words "as we also have forgiven our debtors" (Matthew 6:12) in the Lord's Prayer, we are reminded that Jesus was not giving the power to forgive sins only to the apostles. Rather, in a most special way all of us have the tremendous power and obligation to forgive daily. This tradition is reflected in Scripture all the way back to the last chapter of Genesis, where Joseph in Egypt lovingly forgave his brothers for their attempt to kill him (Genesis 50:15–21).

And why is peace so important? When we are hurt, we can experience bitterness that leads to upset, anger and, consequently, conflict. Paul tells us, "Put away from you all bitterness and wrath and anger and wrangling and slander, together with all malice, and be kind to one another, tenderhearted, forgiving one another, as God in Christ has forgiven you" (Ephesians 4:31–32). Paul wants all of that put away, and instead instructs us in just the opposite—love. We must be kind and tenderhearted. This love goes on into the act of forgiving one another, as God has forgiven us. Paul perfectly outlines ministry conflict at its worst and Jesus' response to it—loving forgiveness.

As mentioned previously, perhaps the ultimate example of forgiveness in Scripture is when Jesus models perfect forgiveness on the cross: "Father, forgive them; for they do not know what they are doing" (Luke 23:34). This first of Jesus' "seven words" on the cross goes to the heart of forgiveness. Jesus forgives because he, like his mother once did, understands the "why." He understands that the people crucifying him do not know what they are doing, nor do they fully understand who they are harming. In our ministry work, many times we are not fully aware of the harm we are doing to each other.

Then we see Jesus do what we must do in forgiving others, "Truly I tell you, today you will be with me in Paradise" (Luke 23:43). In short, we must love. Jesus extends his love to the person on the cross next to him, letting him know the extraordinary good that will come to him this very day. In the midst of our loving forgiveness, extending good wherever we see the possibility is necessary behavior in ministry conflict.

And then with the question, "My God, my God, why have you forsaken me?" (Matthew 27:46), we see the necessary practice in forgiving—asking that question "Why?" It is the same question Mary modeled for us at the temple. Worse than the physical suffering of hanging by nails from the cross as well as the crown of thorns is the psychological hurt of being abandoned in the midst of this horrific pain. Jesus' human spirit has recognized that the Father willed that he endure this pain. He looks for the "why" of this total personal abandonment so as to forgive even his Father.

"When Jesus saw his mother and the disciple whom he loved standing beside her, he said to his mother, 'Woman, here is your son.' Then he said to the disciple, 'Here is your mother'" (John 19:26–27). Jesus returns to the theme of wishing good, of loving others, as part of the process of forgiving. To love is directly the reverse of doing harm. Jesus has nothing to forgive Mary and John; he is simply extending love outwards in the midst of his being harmed. What greater human good could he extend to his mother and John than the gift of each other? "And from that hour the disciple took her into his own home" (John 19:27). In our ministry conflict we must remember daily to return good to those that harm us—and even to those who do not, because there remains the need to not let daily conflicts and hurts take away our energy to extend good wherever we see the opportunity.

Jesus gives the soldiers an opportunity to provide goodness in the midst of the harm they have inflicted on him, to reverse this situation of evil, when he says, "I am thirsty" (John 19:28). In fact, they do respond positively, giving him a sponge full of wine, which not only is a liquid, but a painkiller as well. In our ministry, looking for chances to ask for help from those who harm us reaches at the heart of the conflicts. We teach those who harm us what is the opposite behavior, that of loving and doing good acts.

"It is finished" (John 19:30). In all suffering, there comes an end. It will not last forever. There is an end and a resurrection. There comes to all suffering the peace provided by forgiveness. Jesus' final statement is one of love and resolve, "Father, into your hands I commend my spirit" (Luke 23:46). The suffering is at an end. Jesus has forgiven even his Father and, in trust, commits his final moments into his Father's hands. This is the Father that has allowed all this great mystery of harm against Jesus at the hands of the religious ministers of the time. So in the midst of our suffering at the hands of our fellow-ministers, total trust in God our Father provides the core attitude in forgiving them the suffering we have endured.

• GRATITUDE AND PETITION FOR HELP—COROLLARIES OF LOVING FORGIVENESS

In Jesus' response, thankfulness and humility are corollaries to loving servanthood. Petitioning for light and strength is a corollary to logic. Jesus' third response to conflict, loving forgiveness, has its own corollaries. They are gratitude to God and others and petitions to God for help when resisting the temptation to sin.

The reality of loving forgiveness, which comes from God for our daily sinfulness, makes a strong case for how much God loves us. When God does forgive us, which is immediate upon our request, and our fellow ministers forgive us, gratitude on our part should be a natural phenomenon as we say, "Thank you, God and everyone, for forgiving me when I withheld the good from you." By forgiving, order and peace is restored to the universe. It is once again a kingdom of love.

Regarding petitions to God for help in resisting temptation, Jesus gave us the connection to forgiveness in the daily prayer of the Our Father. Forgiving us our debts as we forgive our debtors is immediately followed by an appeal to the Father to "not bring us to the time of trial," the temptations that cause us to sin in the first place. There is the added petition that God "rescue us from the evil one," which can mean not only the devil, but anyone or anything that holds out those temptations in front of us (Matthew 6:13). Asking for God's help to avoid temptation gets at the root of the whole problem of forgiveness, at least from our side as a sinner. No temptation equals no sin and therefore no need for forgiveness of our debts. But Saint Luke describes the reality in quoting Jesus: "Occasions for stumbling are bound to come, but woe to anyone by whom they come…Be on your guard!" (Luke 17:1, 3).

• PRACTICAL APPLICATIONS OF LOVING FORGIVENESS IN MINISTRY CONFLICT SPIRITUALITY

To practice loving forgiveness on a daily basis requires some specific applications. As in practicing loving servanthood and logic, this third response to ministry conflict will come naturally with practice. We need to stay alert for daily opportunities. We will grow in our own repertoire of ways to practice this special skill of ministry spirituality that Jesus has left us for handling conflict. Here are some suggestions:

- Be aware of feelings of hurt or anger. These feelings let a person know when he has been harmed, and therefore when he needs to forgive.
- Observe the facial expressions of those who harm. Ask yourself: Are they angry, tired or anxious? Try to discern what feeling may have caused the hurtful actions in the first place.
- Another source of information about the "why?" of another's hurtful ways comes by asking the person directly: Why did you say (or do) that hurtful thing?
- Finally, trust your logic and intuition when discerning why another behaved badly.
- Judge whether or not the person acted inadvertently in poor humor or that they are just "clueless."

- After searching for a "why?" that makes forgiveness easier, even though the purpose was negative, look for a way to return good in response to being harmed.
- Pray for them.
- Forgive them.
- Plan to reconcile with those you have harmed.

• LOVING FORGIVENESS AS A SOLUTION TO THE THREE CAUSES OF CONFLICT

Loving forgiveness by its very nature is a practical way to resolve all three causes of conflict. The most prevalent cause of conflict, natural personality differences, is met by loving forgiveness. If one minister doesn't like to be controlled, and another needs to control others, you can experience hurt like the one experienced by Father John in the opening example of this chapter. In knowing Paul's tendency to over-control, John may well have his answer to the "Why?" Any answer that has some logic to it quickly allows Father John to lovingly forgive Paul in his heart, as he prays for forgiveness and strength.

For the emotionally ill side of Paul, Father John can lovingly extend some words of constructive criticism about his behavior. He can then follow it up with a friendly conversation about some aspect of Paul's personal life that Father John knows Paul is concerned about. In other words, he lets Paul know of his loving concern and forgiveness, which gets at the heart of Paul's possible state of anxiety.

Sin presents another challenge for loving forgiveness to resolve. In Father John and Paul's case, there may well be no serious sin. But Paul would need to resolve his actions if he was harboring some grudge against the pastor. Father John's loving forgiveness, followed by his expression of concern, can provide Paul with the motivation to forgive him in turn, leaving Paul's sin behind.

A beautiful summary to this chapter is found in a Psalm:

"For you, O Lord, are good and forgiving,
  abounding in steadfast love to all who call on you" (86:5).

QUESTIONS FOR DISCUSSION

1. In what recent ministry experience did you feel harmed and needed to forgive?

2. Did you recently recognize that you may have harmed someone else? If yes, what took place? What steps have you taken toward reconciliation?

3. How could you put into practice the dictum, "Forgive everyone before you ask the Father for anything"?

CHAPTER NINE

"STAYING STUCK" AND "SPEAKING UP"

In Jesus' spirituality of dealing with ministry conflict, we have witnessed his servanthood, logic and loving forgiveness. But, the Pharisees "stayed stuck" in their natural personality differences with him and in their emotional illness and sins. Their solution to ending the conflict was to stop Jesus from speaking, preaching and healing, and ultimately to kill the prophet. Jesus knew this was their choice. Yet still Jesus attempted to prevent these religious leaders from shackling themselves with the historical responsibility of his crucifixion. He made one last attempt at ending the conflict—that did not involve his death—by trying to speak out publicly, courageously and loudly against them. Today, we too need to use this fourth spiritual avenue to resolve conflict when the first three fail to bring about change.

• HOW WE "STAY STUCK" TODAY

"Staying stuck" means that the natural personality differences, the emotional illness and the sin go on for years, creating the worst damage to ministries. Across the United States dioceses today there may be ministers who are so emotionally ill that they are doing serious harm to others. We have all witnessed how the most egregious illnesses and sins were ignored at the parish and diocesan levels, and the consequential harm it caused innumerable people.

Ongoing problems, whether minor or horrific, at the national, diocesan or parish level, exist simply because ministers "stay stuck," and no one acts to eliminate the problem. Just as the "staying stuck" in the same ministry conflict that caused Jesus to be put on the cross by the religious ministers of his time. Thus, it again puts God on the cross in our own time.

• PUTTING GOD ON THE CROSS

While I was exploring Matthew 23 late one day, I happened to be sitting in a Newman Center chapel. Looking up, I was struck by the figure of Jesus on the cross, which hung over the altar. I felt there was some strong significance I had been missing between that agonized figure and the Pharisees. The only sense I could make of that feeling was that the Pharisees had put Jesus on the cross. But now, as I write this chapter, I see a much stronger significance. It is parallel with our own time. When we as ministry leaders choose to "stay stuck" in our conflict, we are doing the worst of harm to the ministry of the Body of Christ. We may have our brief moments of natural personality differences, emotional illnesses or sins, but if we do not eliminate the conflict, the evil done goes on and on, rippling out like stones thrown into a lake. Like the Pharisees, we too are choosing the solution of killing the prophet, of putting God on the cross.

In our own time, this means to prevent God from working with the subjects of our ministry. For example, God wants to extend love to those who come to our Saint Vincent de Paul ministry for food, clothing, transportation and housing. Through our ministry, these people experience that God does care for them, and loves them, especially in their time of dire need. But if our ministers are racist, these clients do not experience God's love. They only experience more of the hatred and put-downs that they are accustomed to as marginalized people. Our sin of "staying stuck" in racism prevents God's love from being fully experienced through our ministry. God is nailed to the cross and again cannot function.

• WHY WE "STAY STUCK"

Even though natural personality differences, emotional illness and sin cause ministry conflict, these three causes by their very nature can also produce the condition of stagnation. If a minister, out of jealousy and a strong irrational fear of losing his territory, gets locked into a control battle with a new minister, these three causes of conflict create an emotional mindset that is not easily broken. It may have happened to the Pharisees. It can happen to us. Just one of the causes can easily lock us into a long-standing battle. For example, if in fact you are better than me in our area of ministry, and if I already have low self-esteem, my need to protect myself can drive me to irrational and firmly held attitudes and behaviors that prolong conflict.

Other factors that can foster "staying stuck" in conflict:

- simple human weaknesses, such as fear of what like-minded friends will think;
- unwillingness to change once we are involved in something of importance to us;
- lack of insight into our own attitudes and behaviors;
- ignorance of the promptings of the Holy Spirit in our own thinking or in the statements of others;
- irrational level of competitiveness;
- refusal to give up the pleasure sin gives, whether pride or lust;
- general lack of spirituality in one's life;
- unwillingness to look for solutions to personality differences;
- unwillingness to get counseling for anxiety or addiction.

• WHY "STAYING STUCK" RESULTS IN THE DESIRE TO KILL THE PROPHET

In Jesus' situation, the Pharisees were affected by all three causes of conflict in ministry. As to natural personality differences, Jesus was a challenge to their religious control over the Jewish people. Not only was he challenging their teachings, but he performed many miracles that supported his teachings. He said he was the Son of God. All of this challenged the Pharisees' religious "turf." Jesus was a threat to their pride and their authoritarian control. The best that can be said for them is that their belief system was threatened.

• JESUS "SPEAKS UP"

The most notable quote showing how Jesus courageously and forcefully spoke up is in his "Woe to you, scribes and Pharisees, hypocrites!" (Matthew 23:13). In his thorough attack, he repeats this strong summary five more times. "You...hypocrites!" sums up their conflict with Jesus as religious leaders, their emotional irrationality in not practicing what they teach, and in their many sins directly opposed to their status as religious leaders. He also adds: "Woe to you blind guides" (vv. 16 and 24) "You blind fools!" (v. 17), "How blind you are!" (v. 19), "You blind Pharisees!" (v. 26), and "You snakes, you brood of vipers!" (v. 33). How more outspoken and forceful could Jesus' anger have been, all within just twenty verses of Scripture?

This attack by Jesus was verbally forceful. But courage was also evident in that he must have heard of their intent to kill him. Whether through his apostles and their friends in the temple, or from Jesus' friend, the high priest Nicodemus, who would carry out his burial, Jesus faced the Pharisees in the temple and dared to confront them anyway.

In the past, Jesus had confronted the Pharisees, probably even individually, regarding their authority, conflict, irrationality and even their sins. But they were still "stuck" in their ways, even now to the point of intending his death. The three prior ways Jesus sought to resolve his differences with the Pharisees had not worked. So this attack by Jesus presents a much different approach. This is a very public, fact-specific, forceful and courageous approach. Nevertheless, we must note that, intertwined with his attack, he still tries his three basic solutions. Today, this courageous anger is what ministry leadership is called to.

What are the elements of this "speaking up" solution of Jesus?

These four seem the most important: (1) present the facts; (2) go public; (3) be forceful; and (4) be courageous.

Obvious caveats include: (1) Be sure the facts are true and bear the weight of seriousness; (2) Go public only after attempting to resolve the ministry conflict individually (going public can mean going to a higher authority for resolution); (3) Judge the appropriate degree, manner and forcefulness of the anger; and (4) Weigh the consequences of speaking out against the importance of the issue.

The whole issue of the sin of pedophilia presents an extraordinary example of "speaking up" in our own times. Even bishops in the United States kept silent as they moved the predators from one parish to another. Finally, victims made the decision to speak up forcefully and to courageously expose the sin that was so seriously damaging. They presented the facts and, by going public, also broke the silence.

• OTHER SOLUTIONS TO "STAYING STUCK"
Besides the powerful solution of speaking up, modern psychology and sociology provide additional methods for dealing with those who insist on "staying stuck." Professional counseling provides one of the most effective approaches to healing those with serious natural personality differences or emotional illnesses. Getting someone to counseling, however, can be difficult. So a forceful and courageous means of challenging an emotionally ill person might be warranted, including but not limited to, requiring that the person attend counseling until he is cured or his problem is resolved.

Breaking free from remaining stuck in serious sin can likewise be assisted with professional counseling, whether it is lust, pride, greed or some other harm to ministry. The sin may be behavior born from personality-difference conflict or emotional illness, including addictions. If the sin is a fully conscious choice to pursue serious sin for its own sake, then additional assistance in the form of aggressive spiritual direction is needed besides professional counseling. The adjective "aggressive" does not denote the kind of spiritual direction, because that would be the antithesis of true spiritual direction. Rather, it refers to requiring the person stuck in sin to maintain spiritual direction until the condition of sin is resolved.

Additional solutions to a person choosing to stay stuck in that which is seriously harming ministry are (1) to leave the current ministry for another where they can do no harm, (2) leave ministry altogether, or, (3) be removed from ministry. Each of these choices should be a last resort after successes or failures on his or her part to eliminate the personality differences, the emotional illness or the sin. Each of these choices would also be determined by the seriousness of his or her harm to ministry.

• PRACTICAL APPLICATIONS FOR "SPEAKING UP" IN MINISTRY
CONFLICT SPIRITUALITY
Spirituality is more than simply believing and having faith. In order to be truly spiritual, we must live out or speak out about our beliefs. Once we accept the necessity of "speaking up," we need practical applications for our daily use. As you experiment with applying this methodology, you will come up with a growing number of applications that you can use. The following are some suggestions:

- Be sure of the facts about the situation; interview both sides of the conflict; search out all possible circumstances affecting the "staying stuck" minister or ministers.
- Trust your judgment about whether you have sufficiently tried the three solutions of Jesus. If the matter is serious enough, seek counsel to corroborate your judgment.
- Understand the consequences of speaking up. Accordingly, choose a way you believe will be effective in breaking from being stuck.
- Consider a progression based on the problem's seriousness: going up the chain of command, going public verbally or in writing, going to the civil authorities and press.

- Remember this description of Jesus' behavior with the religious ministers and the people in the Temple: it was public, courageous, forceful and angry. Six times he says, "You hypocrites!"
- Pray daily for the Holy Spirit to give you "light and strength," proper judgment and the necessary courage.

We have the historical present-day example of Catholics speaking out on the most serious issue—pedophilia. The only possible excuse for prior cover-ups was general ignorance until the mid-1980s about the incurability of the sickness. Individual victims coming forth and the involvement of civil authorities and the press provided the outrage that ultimately broke the silence in the new millennium. The damage to church ministry, including those who walked away from their faith, is unfathomable.

Yet there is a bright light in all of this. In 2004, the United States Conference of Catholic Bishops chose Illinois Appellate Court Justice Anne M. Burke to head the National Review Board, an independent group of lay Catholics, to investigate and establish a system of holding all United States dioceses to standards that would seek to control the problem of pedophilia. After two-and-a-half years of service on that board, Justice Burke came away with the following primary conclusion, which she presented during a lecture at the College of the Holy Cross in Worcester, Massachusetts, "For me, the days of passive Catholicism are over. This is not so much a political reaction as a spiritual reaction. And, what can be done? Raise some hell for a start. Be vigilant. Be outspoken. Demand transparency" (February 8, 2005).

QUESTIONS FOR DISCUSSION

1. Where have I, or another minister, been stuck in conflict?
2. What solutions seemed to resolve the "being stuck" conflict for myself or for others?
3. Where have I witnessed "speaking up" breaking through "being stuck"?

CHAPTER TEN

THE MINISTRY CONFLICT
SPIRITUALITY OF JESUS

Rachel, the parish religious education director, walks early each morning for an hour in the park. This Catholic minister starts her day with a prayer to her guardian angel and the Memorare to Mary. As she walks she does the readings from that day's Mass in her *Living with Christ* booklet, looking for what strikes her, whether a word or phrase. Reflecting on that word or phrase, Rachel trusts there is some special message for her, and she talks to God about it. She also both enjoys the beauty of the morning sky, and greeting the other walkers in the park. Throughout the walk, Rachel thinks up new ideas for her ministry. Afterward, she goes to the nearby church for early Mass. This daily routine starts her day of ministry. Rachel strongly believes in the promise that God gives light and strength for her ministry work through the Mass. Rachel regularly experiences conflict in her work, partly due to her strong personality. But she practices loving servanthood, logic and loving forgiveness throughout the day. She also spontaneously thanks God often for the peace and beauties of that day of ministry.

This routine of Rachel's describes one minister's practice of the primary commandment of Jesus—to love God and our neighbor as ourselves. She is in a relationship with God through the word of the day's Mass, the sacrament of the Eucharist and the enjoyment of the Father's morning creation. The walk in the park even provides opportunity for serving others in her cheerful greeting and conversation. Then the day of ministry allows her be a loving servant to others, to use her logic in planning and dealing with problems and to lovingly forgive the hurts of the day. Rachel also sees to meeting her own needs by having chosen a leadership position and doing the children's ministry she loves.

• WHAT IS SPIRITUALITY?

Rachel is one example of someone who lives ministry conflict spirituality. In this concluding chapter, we bring together all the wisdom of Jesus we have explored in Matthew 23. Jesus left us with a system for dealing with the conflicts that go on among ministers. In fact, he gives us a complete practical system of spirituality. Our first question then is to define spirituality. One can describe spirituality as simply the living out one's spiritual beliefs.

Living out our beliefs in practice brings us again to Jesus' own summary in the form of his greatest commandments for living:

> "You shall love the Lord your God with all your heart, and with all your soul, and with all your mind, and with all your strength." The second is this, "You shall love your neighbor as yourself." There is no other commandment greater than these (Mark 12:30–31).

Loving God, neighbor and self spell out how our beliefs are to become our spirituality.

• PRACTICING GOD'S WILL AND JOY THROUGH OUR TALENTS

Ministers in their spiritual life worry about doing God's will. They also appreciate a spiritual life that can somehow not be somber in spite of the conflicts of daily ministry. Both needs are superbly met in the same knowing and using of their own unique talents. Identifying and using those talents are so essential to spirituality.

In our relationship with God we consider it important to know the Father's will for our unique life. We ask, "What is our purpose?"

The answer lies in knowing the unique talents with which God endowed us. If God gave us the special talent of leadership, we simply need to use it and that will take up a large portion of what God wants us to do with our life. If we have artistic skill, that needs to take up our time. Those with counseling skills need to use them or God's will becomes frustrated. How do you know your talents and therefore God's will for your life? Notice what you enjoy doing and are good at or can become good at. Then the puzzle is solved, for those are your unique talents from God.

The other side of the talent coin has to do with the emotions of joyful versus somber. Enjoyment, pleasure and joy affect our spirituality when our daily life is also full of enjoyment due to our utilizing our unique talents. God has built this enjoyment into our personality. Even being able to see the humorous side of the ministry conflicts we endure comes from this basic joy in the daily use of our unique, God-given talents.

• RESPONDING TO GOD'S PHYSICAL CREATION

When Jesus used the image of the mother hen in Matthew 23 to represent God's loving forgiveness, he may well have seen that very image many times in Nazareth. In fact, the mother hens may have been protecting their chicks from a town dog or an early morning fox. Jesus noticed and reflected on his Father's creation. Physical creation, whether of God or man, became the stuff of Jesus' spiritual reflections and discourse. Even in challenging the Pharisee leaders, Jesus had observed their fixation on gold versus the temple altar, and the whitened sepulchers of Jerusalem. Connecting our spirituality to the images of the physical creation is also important. Our God puts intelligent meaning and symbol into everything, be it the sun overhead or the shade of the trees. Mostly, God's creations reflect love for us and God's power and artistic intelligence. Like Jesus, we need creation to be a constant source of spiritual connection with God, neighbor and ourselves.

• GIFTS AND FRUITS OF THE HOLY SPIRIT

Though our topics here are the gifts and fruits from God, and not something of our own making or efforts, we can nevertheless be thankful for their existence and pray to receive them. The gifts of the Holy Spirit are skills most needed in resolving ministry conflicts. Isaiah first describes them in a reference to Christ:

> "The spirit of the LORD shall rest on him,
>> the spirit of wisdom and understanding,
>> the spirit of counsel and might [fortitude],
>> the spirit of knowledge [and piety, an addition of Church
>> tradition] and the fear of the LORD." (Isaiah 11:2)

Since these seven gifts are from God, the Holy Spirit of Truth, we receive all these guides to our intelligence in order to discern and follow through on truth. We need these backups to our efforts of servanthood, logic, forgiveness and the courageous anger required to speak up. We must pray often for these gifts from God.

We again need to pray for the fruits of the Holy Spirit from God. Saint Paul lists these: "The fruit of the Spirit is love, joy, peace, patience, kindness, generosity, faithfulness, gentleness, and self-control" (Galatians 5:22–23). Church tradition adds three more: goodness, modesty and chastity. We might even suggest that these are signs of God the Holy Spirit's presence in a minister. If these signs are present, we know where these qualities may well be coming from and can thank God for them in our fellow ministers or even in ourselves. We must make efforts to live these qualities. But at the same time we need to pray for these very helpful fruits or gifts of the Holy Spirit's presence within us as we deal with ministry conflict.

• THE MASS AND SACRAMENTS

The Mass sums up everything about our ministry conflict spirituality. At the heart of the Mass is God's love for us, whether in our redemption or in Jesus' real presence in the Eucharist. We enter into conversation with God in our prayers and God with us in the word. We do this in community with our neighbors, all the mystical body members, with whom we are in peace. Only that cross over or near the altar reminds us of the conflict that happens in ministry. We receive that promised light and strength to help us in our ministry as we offer our work to the Father along with the sacrifice of Jesus. The graces of light and strength we come away with may include gifts and fruits from the loving Holy Spirit within us. That light and strength make it possible to continue the loving servanthood, logic, loving forgiveness and speaking up that Jesus and Mary have modeled for us.

All seven sacraments invigorate our ministry. Through baptism and confirmation we enter into a personal relationship with God and a service to our fellow members of God's family. Penance and the Eucharist provide the forgiveness for our daily sins and conflict, and provide the food by which we live our love relationship with God and others. Each day we can receive this food, this nourishment, to maintain us in our ministry and its conflicts. The sacrament of the anointing of the sick provides that final act of trust in the Father at the end of all human conflict as we are about to say with Jesus, "It is finished" (John 19:13).

• THE REST OF DAILY LIFE

Besides the conversations with God that make up the Mass and the sacraments, the minister's entire ministry needs such conversation. When we are up or down, God wants us to share that and understand that God hears every word and both enjoys our successes and shares our concerns. Our daily ministry life and its conflicts are even more God's concerns than they are ours. "Your kingdom come. / Your will be done, on earth as it is in heaven. / Give us this day our daily bread. / And forgive us our debts, as we also have forgiven our debtors. / And do not bring us to the time of trial, but rescue us from the evil one" (Matthew 6:10–13).

Our relationships and conflicts and how we handle them should be no different from how we deal with our parishioners, our relatives, our friends and the wider community.

• WHY THE MINISTRY CONFLICT? WHY THE CROSS?

One morning a minister may wake up and think, "Are all the conflicts and difficulties of my ministry worth it?" Jesus, with his human nature, could well have asked the same question. The answer we have to presume is a one-word answer: Yes. Followed by another one-word reason: Love. Jesus so loves the Father and he so loves us that he endures the conflicts, the trials and the ultimate sacrifice. This should be our answer also.

But an additional answer lies in the nature of ministry conflict. Ministry conflict comes out of the reality of who we are. Human beings are capable, because of our free will, of doing the good that God expects and evil as well. Just like two cars colliding in the middle of an intersection, so also the unintentional or intentional harming of another person just happens in ministry.

We have seen the three causes of ministry conflicts: natural personality differences, emotional illness and sin. There is no avoiding these three very human causes, even every day. Even the reality of apparent failure, as happened to Jesus on the cross, can also be our lot in ministry. So the final solution is that simple trust, submitting even the apparent failure into the Father's hands. That trust comes from knowing God loves us and always brings about an ultimate good conclusion to our loving efforts.

What better way to live out our spiritual beliefs in our ministry than by following Jesus and his steadfast example of loving servanthood, logic, forgiveness and courage all the way to the cross? What better way to simply live out our beliefs in all the behaviors of our daily life and spirituality?

QUESTIONS FOR DISCUSSION

1. What are some beliefs that I want to live out in how I deal with ministry conflict?

2. What are some practical applications of Jesus' solutions that I would like to practice?

3. What new short prayer would I like to say each day that summarizes how I want God to help me behave in ministry conflict situations?

BIBLIOGRAPHY

Aquinas, Thomas. *St. Thomas Aquinas: Summa Theologica.* Fathers of the English Dominican Province, trans. Notre Dame, Ind.: Christian Classics, 1981.

Bacik, James J. *Tensions in the Church: Facing the Challenges, Seizing the Opportunities.* Kansas City, Mo.: Sheed and Ward, 1993.

Barry, William A., and William J. Connolly. *The Practice of Spiritual Direction.* San Francisco: HarperSanFrancisco, 1986.

_____. *Finding God in All Things: A Companion to the Spiritual Exercises of St. Ignatius.* Notre Dame, Ind.: Ave Maria, 1991.

Bausch, William J. *The Total Parish Manual: Everything You Need to Empower Your Faith Community.* Mystic, Conn.: Twenty-Third Publications, 1994.

Brennan, Patrick. *The Way of Forgiveness: How to Heal Life's Hurts and Restore Broken Relationships.* Cincinnati: Servant, 2000.

Brown, Raymond E. *An Introduction to New Testament Christology.* Mahwah, N.J.: Paulist, 1994.

Brown, Richard. *A Practical Guide for Starting an Adult Faith Formation Program.* San Jose, Calif.: Resource Publications, Inc., 2003.

Buby, Bertrand. *Mary of Galilee: Mary in the New Testament. Vol. 1.* New York: Alba House, 1994.

Burke, John. *A Good News Spirituality: Finding Holiness in Parish Life.* Mahwah, N.J.: Paulist, 2000.

Chittister, Joan D. *Heart of Flesh: A Feminist Spirituality for Women and Men.* Grand Rapids: Wm. B. Eerdmans, 1998.

Comer, Ronald J. *Fundamentals of Abnormal Psychology.* New York: Worth, 2004.

Connell, Martin, ed. *The Catechetical Documents: A Parish Resource.* Chicago: Liturgy Training Publications, 1996.

Crosby, Michael H. *The Dysfunctional Church: Addiction and Codependency in the Family of Catholicism.* Notre Dame, Ind.: Ave Maria, 1991.

Delio, Ilia. *Simply Bonaventure: An Introduction to His Life Thought and Writings.* Hyde Park, N.Y.: New City, 2003.

Dougherty, Rose Mary. *Group Spiritual Direction: Community for Discernment.* Mahwah, N.J.: Paulist, 1995.

Dyckman, Katherine Marie and L. Patrick Carroll, *Inviting the Mystic, Supporting the Prophet: An Introduction to Spiritual Direction.* Mahwah, N.J.: Paulist, 1981.

Gillen, Marie A. and Maurice C. Taylor, eds. *Adult Religious Education: A Journey of Faith Development.* Mahwah, N.J.: Paulist, 1995.

Gillespie, C. Kevin. *Psychology and American Catholicism.* New York: Crossroad, 2001.

Greeley, Andrew M. *The Catholic Revolution: New Wine, Old Wineskins, and the Second Vatican Council.* Berkeley, Calif.: University of California Press, 2004.

Green, Thomas H. *Come Down Zacchaeus: Spirituality and the Laity.* Notre Dame, Ind.: Ave Marie, 1988.

Greenleaf, Robert. *Servant Leadership: A Journey into the Nature of Legitimate Power and Greatness.* Larry Spears, ed. Mahwah, N.J.: Paulist, 2002.

Groeschel, Benedict J. *The Courage to Be Chaste.* Mahwah, N.J.: Paulist, 1985.

Gula, Richard M. *Ethics in Pastoral Ministry.* Mahwah, N.J.: Paulist, 1995.

Haring, Bernard. *My Hope for the Church: Critical Encouragement for the Twenty-First Century.* Peter Heinegg, trans. Liguori, Mo.: Liguori/Triumph, 1999.

Hart, Thomas N. *The Art of Christian Listening.* Mahwah, N.J.: Paulist, 1980.

Heney, David. *Motivating Your Parish to Change: Concrete Leadership Strategies for Pastors, Administrators and Lay Leaders.* San Jose, Calif.: Resource Publications, 1998.

Johnson, Richard. *A Christian's Guide to Mental Wellness.* Liguori, Mo.: Liguori Publications, 1990.

Johnston, William. *Mystical Theology: The Science of Love.* Maryknoll, N.Y.: Orbis, 1998.

Kaufman, Philip S. *Why You Can Disagree and Remain a Faithful Catholic.* New York: Crossroad, 1995.

Kavanaugh, Kieran, and Otilio Rodriguez, trans. *The Collected Works of St. John of the Cross.* Washington, D.C.: ICS Publications, 1991.

_____. *The Collected Works of St. Teresa of Avila, Volume One.* Washington, D.C.: ICS Publications, 1987.

Keating, Thomas. *Open Mind, Open Heart: The Contemplative Dimension of the Gospel.* New York: Continuum, 1994.

Knaus, Dr. William J. *Do It Now: How to Stop Procrastinating.* Englewood Cliffs, N.J.: Prentice Hall, 1979.

Küng, Hans, *On Being a Christian.* New York: Image, 1984.

Lieberman, David J. *Never Be Lied To Again: How to Get the Truth in 5 Minutes or Less in Any Conversation or Situation.* New York: St. Martin's, 1999.

Linn, Matthew, and Dennis Linn. *Healing Life's Hurts: Healing Memories Through the Five Stages of Forgiveness.* Mahwah, N.J.: Paulist, 1993.

Lyons, Enda. *Jesus: Self-Portrait by God.* New York: Columba, 2004.

Mahoney, John. *The Making of Moral Theology: A Study of Roman Catholic Tradition (The Martin D'Arcy Memorial Lectures 1981-2).* New York: Oxford University Press, 1989.

Maloney, H. Newton. *The Psychology of Religion for Ministry.* Mahwah, N.J.: Paulist, 1995.

May, Gerald G. *Addiction and Grace.* San Francisco: HarperSanFrancisco, 1991.

_____.*Care of Mind, / Care of Spirit.* San Francisco: HarperSanFrancisco, 1992.

McBrien, Richard P. *Catholicism: New Study Edition—Completely Revised and Updated.* San Francisco: HarperSanFrancisco, 1981.

McKinney, Mary Benet. *Sharing Wisdom: A Process for Group Decision Making.* Notre Dame, Ind.: Ave Maria, 1986.

Megargee, Edwin Inglee. *The California Psychological Inventory Handbook.* San Francisco: Jossey-Bass, 1977.

Merton, Thomas. *New Seeds of Contemplation.* New York: New Directions, 1961.

National Conference of Catholic Bishops. *Hispanic Ministry: Three Major Documents.* Washington, D.C.: United States Catholic Conference, 1995.

Peck, M. Scott. *The Different Drum: Community Making and Peace.* New York: Simon and Schuster, 1987.

_____. *People of the Lie: The Hope for Healing Human Evil,* New York: Simon and Schuster, 1983.

Powell, John. *Why Am I Afraid to Love? Overcoming Rejection and Indifference.* Niles, Ill.: Argus, 1972.

Rahner, Karl. *The Need and the Blessing of Prayer,* Bruce W. Gillette, trans. Collegeville, Minn.: Liturgical Press, 1997.

Rausch, Thomas P. *Authority and Leadership in the Church: Past Directions and Future Possibilities.* Collegeville, Minn.: Liturgical Press, 1988.

Reader's Digest. *Know Your Rights: And How to Make Them Work for You.* Pleasantville, N.Y.: Reader's Digest, 1998.

Robbins, Anthony. *Awaken the Giant Within: How to Take Immediate Control of Your Mental, Emotional, Physical and Financial Destiny.* New York: Free Press, 1992.

Rodriguez, Otilio and Kieran Kavanaugh, trans. *The Collected Works of St. John of the Cross.* Washington, D.C.: ICS Publications, 1991.

_____. *The Collected Works of St. Teresa of Avila, Volume Two.* Washington, D.C.: ICS Publications, 1980.

Ryan, Thomas. *Fasting Rediscovered: A Guide to Health and Wholeness for Your Body-Spirit.* Mahwah, N.J.: Paulist, 1981.

Sack, Steven Mitchell. *The Working Woman's Legal Survival Guide: Know Your Workplace Rights Before It's Too Late.* Paramus, N.J.: Prentice Hall Press, 1998.

Sande, Ken. *The Peacemaker: A Biblical Guide to Resolving Personal Conflict.* Grand Rapids: Baker, 2004.

Shawchuck, Norman. *How to Manage Conflict in the Church: Conflict Interventions and Resouces.* Leith, N.D.: Spiritual Growth Resources, 1983.

Sheldrake, Philip. *Spirituality and History: Questions of Interpretation and Method, 2nd ed.* Maryknoll, N.Y.: Orbis, 1998.

United States Catholic Conference, Inc.—Libreria Editrice Vaticana, *Catechism of the Catholic Church.* New York: Sadlier, 1994.

Weigel, George. *Courage to Be Catholic: Crisis, Reform and the Future of the Church.* New York: Basic Books, 2004.

Whitehead, Evelyn Eaton, and James D. Whitehead. *Seasons of Strength: New Visions of Adult Christian Maturing.* Winona, Minn.: Saint Mary's Press, 1995.

INDEX

A

accusations, unjust, 56
addictions, as source of scandal,
    51–53
ageism, 51
alcoholism, 44, 52–53
anger, as symptom of emotional ill-
    ness, 39–40
anxiety, as symptom of emotional
    illness, 9–10, 19, 40
artistic intelligence, 35
        of God, 101
Aquinas, Saint Thomas, 12, 48
Ascent of Mount Carmel, The (John
    of the Cross), 75

C

codependence, 52, 53
communication
        importance of, 8
lack of, 2
computer addictions, 54
counsel, 35–36
courage, lack of, 53, 59

D

decision making, 33
depression, as symptom of emo-
    tional illness, 10, 40–41
dialogue
        importance of, 2–3
drug abuse, 52–53

E

embezzlement, 53
emotional health, 37. *See also* emo-
    tional illness under ministry con-
    flict, sources of

emotional illness, 2. *See also* entry
    under ministry conflict, sources
    of
        impact of, 41–43
        of Pharisees, 20
        signs of, 9–10, 39–41
enmity, 58–59
envy, 56–57
extroverts, 7

F

factions, 54–56
flexibility, 36
forgiveness, 20–22
        Jesus as model for, 85–86
        of God, 21
        practical applications, 88–89
        in Scripture, 82–87
        as solution to ministry con-
            flict, 89

G

gambling, 52–53
God's will, practicing, 100–101
gratitude, 87–88. *See also* thankful-
    ness
greed, 17, 52, 95
"groupies," 51–52

H

hatred, 56–57
Holy Spirit
        fruits of, 102
        gifts of, 102
Jesus on, 76–77, 85
humility, 65–66, 77

I

Interior Castle, The (Teresa of Avila), 75
introverts, 7
intuition, 35
irrational behavior, as symptom of emotional illness, 9, 40–41

J

jealousy, 57. *See also* envy
Jesus
    challenges to hypocrisy, 51
    courageous anger, 23, 94
    on forgiveness, 82–87
    on Holy Spirit, 76–77, 85
    on humility, 66
    on hypocrisy, 18
    leadership style of, 15–16, 25, 66
    on love for neighbor, 63
    as model, 103
    ministry of, 67
    ministry conflict spirituality of, 99–104
    on providence of God, 65
    on servanthood, 61–63
    on sloth, 54
    use of logic, 78–79
John, Saint, 86
John of the Cross, Saint, 75, 76
joy, 101

L

Last Supper, as image of servant-hood, 62
lay ministers, 46
lies, 57–58
logic, 20, 34
    importance of, 74–76

practical applications, 78–79
in Scripture, 76–77
loving forgiveness. *See* forgiveness
loving servanthood. *See* servant-hood
lust, 51–53, 95

M

Mary
    challenges to Jesus, 25
    Jesus' love for, 86
    forgiveness of Jesus, 84
    as model, 103
Mass, 102–103
mediation, 3
micromanagement, 74
ministry conflict
    avoiding reality of, 22–23, 44–46
    reasons for, 104
    solutions to, 2
    acceptance, 8
    admonishment, 13
    communication, 8
    forgiveness, 89
    maintaining emotional health of staff, 11
    prayer, 12
    recognition of potential conflicts, 8, 10–11
    setting a good example, 12–13
    sources of, 2
    emotional illness, 8–10, 16–17
    personality differences, 6–7, 15–16
    sin, 12–13, 17–18
    spirituality of Jesus, 99–104

N

negligence, 53–54

nurturance, 36

O

ongoing formation, 3

organizational skills, 33–34

Our Father, 65, 103

  forgiveness in, 84, 87–88

overreaction, avoiding, 43

P

parish staff

  factions among, 55–56

  frustrations of, 73

  role of, ix

  screening, x

  dismissal of, 5, 22, 42, 50–51

Paul, Saint, 48, 54, 57, 65, 66, 70, 83, 102

personality conflict. *See* personality differences

personality differences. *See* entry under ministry conflict, sources of

personality skills, 25–28

  identifying, 28–31

  role in conflict, 31–37

pride, 49–50, 66–67, 95

procrastination, 53–54

R

racism, 51, 92

responsibility

  to God, 66–67

trait of, 34

S

sacraments, 102–103

scandal, 51–53

self-esteem, unhealthy, 21, 58

self-indulgence, 17–18

servanthood

  attitude of, 3, 18–19

  difficulties in, 69–70

  God's, 64–65

  practical applications, 63–64

  as preference for the poor, 67–68

  in Scripture, 61–63

  as solution to conflict, 68–69

sexism, 51

shared vision

  lack of, 2

shared spirituality, 3

sin

  as cause of ministry conflict, 12–13, 17–18, 48–59

  conquering through servant-hood, 19

  courage, lack of, 53

  defined, 47

  enmity, 58–59

  envy, 56–57

  greed, 51–53

  hatred, 56–57

  injustice, 50–51, 56

  lies, 57–58

  list of, 38

  lust, 51–53

  negligence, 53–54

  pride, 49–50, 66–67

  procrastination, 53–54

  scandal, 51–53

  slander, 57–58

  sloth, 53–54

  strife, 58–59

slander, 57–58

sociability, 33

"speaking up"
    practical applications, 9697
    as solution to "staying stuck,"
      94–95
spirituality, defined, 100
"staying stuck." *See also* ministry
  conflict, avoiding reality of
    reasons for, 92–93
    results of, 93–94
    solutions to, 95–96
    speaking up against, 94–95
    ways for, 91–92
strife, 58–59

T
talents, discernment of, 101
television addiction, 54
Teresa of Avila, Saint, 75, 76
thankfulness, 65, 77
theft, 73
tolerance, 37